Teaching English Overseas

A Job Guide For Americans and Canadians

Jeff Mohamed

Third Edition, Revised

English International Publications

Published by English International Publications
www.english-international.com

© 2003 by Jeff Mohamed

First Published 2000
Third, revised edition 2003

ISBN 0-9677062-6-2

About The Author

Jeff Mohamed has been involved in TEFL (Teaching English as a Foreign Language) for well over 30 years. His TEFL career, which began in France in 1968, includes:

- teaching students of over 80 nationalities in 7 countries;
- teaching over 130 TEFL Certificate and Diploma courses in Spain, Egypt, the UK and the USA;
- giving TEFL-training lectures, workshops and short courses in 17 countries;
- directing EFL schools and TEFL-training centers in Spain, Libya, England and the USA.

For several years Jeff directed International House London, at that time the largest TEFL training center in the world. He also directed I.H.'s Central Department, which was responsible for recruiting several hundred teachers each year to work in 70 affiliated schools around the world.

Born and educated in England, Jeff has lived and worked in the USA since 1990. From 1993 through 1998, he was the Joint Chief Assessor responsible for monitoring standards in all RSA/Cambridge CELTA (Certificate in English Language Teaching to Adults) centers in Canada, the USA and Latin America. During this time he also directed and taught the RSA/Cambridge CELTA program offered at English International in San Francisco.

Jeff currently directs English International, a company that publishes TEFL materials and offers distance learning TEFL programs. He also teaches CELTA and ESL courses at North Harris College in Houston, Texas.

Disclaimer

This book is designed to provide information in regard to the subject matter covered. It is sold with the understanding that the publisher and the author are not engaged in rendering legal or other professional services. If legal or other professional assistance is required, the services of a competent professional should be sought.

Every effort has been made to ensure that this guide is as accurate as possible. However, there may be mistakes both typographical and in content. Furthermore, this guide contains information on teaching English overseas only up to the date of printing.

The purpose of this guide is to educate, inform and entertain. The author and the publisher shall have neither liability nor responsibility to any person or entity with respect to any loss or damage caused, or alleged to be caused, directly or indirectly by the information or opinions contained in this book.

If you do not wish to be bound by the above, you should contact the publisher within 30 days of your receipt of the book to request a full refund.

Preface

For a variety of reasons, English has become the most widely spoken language in the world and is used to some extent or other by more than one billion people. In addition to being the first language in many countries, English is now the international language of trade, science, tourism, aviation, diplomacy and computers. Given current economic and political realities and the incredible growth of the Internet, there can be no doubt that demand for instruction in English as a second or foreign language will continue to increase for the foreseeable future.

This is very good news for those of us who have English as our first language and want to work overseas, because most people who wish to learn English want to learn it from a native speaking teacher. It is also particularly good news for native speakers of Canadian and US English because North American English is now the most popular variety of the language with learners around the world.

If you are a reasonably educated native speaker of North American English, you should have little or no difficulty finding a teaching job in most areas of the world. However, working as a teacher of English overseas carries with it risks as well as rewards: teaching itself is not for everyone, living abroad is frequently very challenging, and not all overseas jobs are good jobs!

While this book is primarily aimed at people who want to live and work overseas for only a year or two, I hope that it will encourage at least some readers to make teaching English a career. Whatever your reasons for wanting to teach English overseas, I hope that this book will help you to find suitably rewarding employment in the country of your choice.

Jeff Mohamed
Houston, Texas
May 2003

5

Table Of Contents

CHAPTER 8
LEGALITIES, PRACTICALITIES & HEALTH

CHAPTER 9
DEALING WITH A NEW CULTURE

Chapter 1

FAQ's About Teaching English Overseas

SOME FREQUENTLY ASKED QUESTIONS

If you are thinking about teaching English overseas, you probably have some basic questions which you would like answered. The questions below are just some of those which I have been asked many times over the years or which frequently appear on Internet discussion boards.

I have tried to answer each question accurately but briefly. However, in many cases, you can find a much fuller answer in a later chapter of this book. Where this is so, I have added a reference to the pages where you can find a more comprehensive response.

What are the differences between TEFL, TESL, TESOL and ELT?

TEFL (Teaching English as a Foreign Language) involves teaching people, usually in their own country, who want to use English for business, leisure, travel, etc.

TESL refers to the Teaching of English as a Second Language and it involves teaching immigrants in English-speaking countries.

TESOL (Teaching English to Speakers of Other Languages) and *ELT* (English Language Teaching) are terms which cover both TEFL and TESL. Confusingly, the acronym *TESOL* is also used to refer to the American professional association: Teachers of English to Speakers of Other Languages.

Are there really jobs out there? Where are they?

There are many more TEFL jobs worldwide than there are native-speaking EFL teachers. If you are American or Canadian, you should be able to find jobs reasonably easily in Latin America, Asia, and Eastern or Central Europe. The only markets which will be difficult to break into will be those in other English-speaking countries, Western Europe (unless you have a European Union passport), and Africa.

See pages 51-62.

Where are the highest paying jobs?

The highest paying jobs in Asia are in Japan and Korea. Elsewhere, the best salaries are paid by employers in the oil-producing countries of the Arabian Gulf.

See pages 51-62.

Do I need a degree to be able to teach EFL overseas?

A degree is almost always preferred by employers, but it is not legally essential in most countries. However, it is impossible to work legally in some parts of Asia and the Mid East without a degree.

See pages 23-24.

Has the job market changed since 9/11 and the invasion of Iraq?

Not really but you should monitor political developments if you are thinking of teaching in Mid Eastern or other Moslem countries.

Do I need specific TEFL training or certification?

No ... and yes! A lot of schools employ untrained teachers and some of those teachers do just fine. However, most good employers now require or at least prefer teachers to be both trained and certified. So if you want a good job, particularly in the more competitive markets, you should seriously consider taking a TEFL certificate training course.

See pages 24-27.

How long does TEFL training take?

TEFL training and certification can be obtained quite quickly. Even the most widely recognized TEFL certificate, the Cambridge CELTA, can be obtained in only four weeks. Many other TEFL certificate courses can also be completed in 4 weeks (or part-time over 3-18 months). Some even shorter training courses are available but they are rarely recognized by more reputable employers overseas.

See pages 31-43.

Can I obtain TEFL certification via distance learning?

Several distance courses are available. The best of these provide a good introduction to TEFL and can be very helpful with obtaining employment. However, if you want to be able to compete successfully for jobs with teachers who have taken a face-to-face TEFL certificate course, you should choose a distance course that lasts at least 100 hours and includes at least six hours of evaluated practice teaching. (The latter is normally carried out via the video-recording of lessons.)

See pages 43-44.

Which is the best TEFL training course?

A lot of courses offer adequate or good training. However, some TEFL certificates are not recognized by employers overseas. The most widely recognized certificate available in North America is the Cambridge CELTA (also referred to as the RSA/Cambridge CELTA). This is partly because CELTA courses are very closely monitored by Cambridge University to insure that they provide high quality training.

See pages 36-39.

Do I need to know a foreign language?

Almost all TEFL jobs require you to teach English purely in English, and so knowledge of a foreign language is not essential. However, having some experience of foreign language learning will give you useful insights into what language is and how we learn it, and studying a foreign language will help you to learn more about English, and

15

particularly English grammar. Also, knowledge of the language of the country where you work will make your out-of-work life easier and more rewarding.

Do I need to be a certain age?

No. I have known teachers as young as 18 and as old as 75 who have found jobs overseas. However, it is often difficult to get a job if you are under 21, and it also tends to be more difficult if you are over about 50-55. Some countries have compulsory retirement ages.

Can I teach EFL if English is not my native language?

Yes, if your spoken and written English is of a very high level. Having a slight accent is not a problem, but you need to be able to express yourself fluently and accurately in both speech and writing. (Having a "foreign" accent will be a significant drawback if you have not undergone specific TEFL training, since all that most untrained EFL teachers really have to offer employers is their ability to model native speaker pronunciation.)

Can I bring a partner overseas with me?

If you obtain a job and a residence visa, you can usually obtain a residence visa for a wife or husband, but not for any other kind of partner. However, he/she probably will not be allowed to work and most entry-level TEFL jobs do not pay enough to allow you to support a nonworking dependent. If your partner is involved in TEFL, you should both be able to find jobs in the same place, particularly if you apply to large schools or for jobs in bigger cities.

Can I bring children with me?

If you obtain a job and a residence visa, you will certainly be able to obtain a residence visa for your children. However, you should realize that most entry-level TEFL jobs do not pay high enough salaries to enable single parents to support children. Married couples in which both partners teach EFL may be able to support children overseas, though.

Can I arrange a job before leaving home?

For many countries, it is possible to arrange a job in advance, if you have a degree and a reputable TEFL certificate. Unless you are just looking for very short-term jobs, I would recommend that you try to fix up a job in advance.

See pages 68-69.

How can I arrange a job overseas?

Some people travel to their target country to look for work. Others arrange a job in advance either by answering job advertisements or by contacting possible employers. Advice and information on both approaches to job searching are included in this book.

See pages 67-72.

Where can I find addresses of overseas schools?

Appendix 5 has a list of more than 400 overseas schools. English International also produces a PC disk with the addresses of more than 1400 overseas employers.

See pages 141-220.

How can I be sure that an overseas employer is reputable?

Accept a job only if it is with an organization which has an established reputation or which is known to someone whose opinion you trust. Check what other people say about the employer on Internet discussion sites. Ask the potential employer to put you in touch with a current or past employee.

Before accepting any job offer, use the checklist given in Chapter 6 to make sure that the conditions of work are reasonable.

See pages 85-88.

When do jobs start?

In Europe, most jobs start in September/October, with a much smaller number becoming available in January. Outside of those months, it is extremely difficult to find work. Elsewhere in the world, jobs are generally available at any time of the year.

How long will I have to commit to?

Most good jobs require that you sign a year's contract. This is almost always true of jobs which can be arranged in advance and which provide airfare and housing. However, if you travel overseas to arrange a job, it is often possible to work on a month-by-month basis.

A few government-sponsored programs, such as the Peace Corps and the JET Program, require a two year commitment.

Can I teach without a work permit or residence visa?

To live and work in a foreign country, you must have a work permit; this then enables you to get a residence visa. To do even short-term work or private teaching overseas without a valid work permit is a criminal offense in all countries, and offenders may be imprisoned or deported.

In reality, the degree of risk involved varies greatly from country to country. Americans and Canadians who teach illegally in parts of Asia, Latin America and Western Europe rarely seem to have major problems, provided that they do not stay for more than three months.

See pages 91-93.

How do I get a work permit and residence visa?

Normally, you first have to secure a job offer. Then your employer will sponsor your application for the necessary papers. In most cases, the employer will actually deal with all of the bureaucracy for you.

See pages 91-93.

What are typical working conditions?

In most countries, you can expect to teach a 5-day week of about 20-25 hours. (Of course, this does not include the time you will need to spend on planning your lessons!) Typically, you may have 6-8 weeks of paid holidays and vacations. In the higher-paying Asian countries such as Japan and Korea, you may be required to teach 6 days and 35 hours a week, and you may have as few as 2 weeks a year of paid holidays and vacations.

See pages 51-62.

Will I be paid in dollars?

No. In virtually all overseas TEFL jobs, you will be paid in local currency, not in dollars.

How much will I earn?

It is impossible to answer this because salaries and currency exchange rates vary so much. Also, salary figures are meaningless unless you know the cost of living in each country. For example, a salary of $80 a month in Romania may sound pitiful, but it will actually allow you to live a lot better than a monthly salary of $1000 in Japan or Sweden.

In most countries, entry-level TEFL jobs with reputable employers allow you to live reasonably well (in local terms). They also allow you to do one of two things: to make modest savings or to enjoy your weekends and vacations. Only a few countries offer jobs which allow you to live well, save money and really enjoy your leisure time.

See pages 51-62.

Will I be able to send money home?

If you teach in some Asian or Mid Eastern countries, you are likely to be able to save really significant amounts of money ($500-$1500 a month), and to be allowed to send it home. In most other countries, you will not be able to save so much, and exchange control regulations may make it difficult to send home any savings.

What about taxes?

You will normally pay income tax and social security charges to the government of the country where you work, and in most cases these taxes will be much lower than those in Canada or the USA. You will probably need to file an income form in your home country but you will usually not have to pay any additional Canadian or US taxes on the money which you earned overseas, provided that you stay abroad for at least a year.

Can I teach extra lessons privately?

Most overseas contracts specifically state that you cannot teach privately without the express permission of your employer. However, most employers will allow you to do some private teaching provided that your contract teaching is going well and that you do not steal students from your employer.

What about travel and housing?

If you arrange a job in advance and sign a contract for a year, overseas employers will often pay all or part of your airfare, particularly if the job is in Asia or the Mid East.

In Asia and the Mid East, employers almost always provide housing free or at nominal cost to employees who have arranged jobs from North America. In most other parts of the world, employers may help you to find suitable housing but they will not pay for it.

The standard of housing available varies but it is usually reasonably good in local terms. However, you need to bear in mind that very few countries have housing that matches the standard of housing in the USA or Canada. You should also realize that single-person housing is fairly rare overseas and so teachers often have to share houses or apartments with other teachers.

See pages 52-62.

Do jobs include health insurance?

Most countries have national health services, and you will be eligible to use these as soon as you legally start work. It is often possible, at comparatively little extra cost, to subscribe to some type of local HMO or private health program as well as, or instead of, the local national health service. Any overseas employer who offers you a TEFL job should give you full details of the health insurance situation in the country where you will be living.

See page 98.

Who will my students be?

Most entry-level TEFL jobs involve teaching groups of adults, teenagers and/or younger learners in private language schools. Some jobs require you to teach classes in local junior high schools, high schools or colleges. In some jobs, you may teach mainly or solely individual executives or groups of employees on their companies' premises.

See pages 52-62.

What happens if I really hate the job or the country?

Employers rarely want to keep teachers who are very unhappy. They will normally allow you to terminate your contract early provided that you wait a few weeks until they can arrange a replacement teacher. However, you may be asked to repay all or part of your airfare and of other costs which the employer met on your behalf.

If the employer does not agree to terminate your employment early, you can break your contract by walking off the job and leaving the country. However, this is clearly a very unprofessional approach. It will also make it difficult for you to obtain other TEFL jobs in the future.

In my experience, teachers who end up in totally unsuitable jobs or countries do so because they fail to do enough research before going overseas. If you research jobs and countries carefully, you should be able to avoid serious problems.

Is it possible to build a real career in TEFL?

Most EFL teachers stay in the field for only 1-2 years and then return home to move into other types of work. However, some teachers do make TEFL their main career. In some cases, they settle permanently in an overseas country, often becoming school directors or directors of studies. More frequently, they eventually return to their home country and work in either TEFL or TESL as teachers, trainers, materials writers, program directors, etc.

As the TEFL/TESL market in North America is very competitive, Canadians and Americans who want good long-term positions back home usually find that they need to obtain an MA TESOL degree at some point in their career.

Can you recommend some good books about teaching EFL?

You will find a list of recommended books on TEFL methodology and language development in Chapter 2.

See pages 27-30.

How can I get in touch with other EFL teachers?

Probably the easiest way to contact other EFL teachers around the world is through the Jobs Discussion page of Dave's ESL Cafe website (www.eslcafe.com/jd/) or other similar Internet sites. However, you need to read the postings with a critical eye because many of them are very long on opinion or prejudice but very short on fact!

See page 127.

Chapter 2

Teaching Without TEFL Training

- **Teaching Without A Degree**
- **Teaching With A Degree**
- **Being A Native Speaker Is Not Enough**

TEACHING WITHOUT A DEGREE

Teaching Without A Degree And Without Training

As a native speaker of English, you may be able to find work teaching English overseas even if you have no formal educational qualifications or training. However, your employment options will be extremely limited. You will have to travel overseas at your own expense and risk to look for work, rather than being able to arrange a job from your home country. Also, you almost certainly will be limited to working illegally and for the very worst types of employers.

So, in practical terms, you really need to have either a college degree or specific TEFL training.

Teaching Without A Degree

While it is possible to teach EFL in many countries without a college degree, the lack of a degree will place very severe limitations on your employment possibilities. Most reputable employers refuse to recruit teachers who do not have a BA/BS degree or an equivalent (e.g., BFA). In addition, an increasing number of countries are refusing to issue work permits to people who do not have degrees.

So, the lack of a degree may not be a serious problem if your aim is just to travel around the world, on tourist visas, picking up TEFL jobs here and there for a few weeks at a time to make some extra money. But it is going to make it impossible for you to obtain longer-term, legal work in many countries.

If you want to find longer-term legal work overseas but do not want to do/complete a degree first, you should definitely consider obtaining a TEFL certificate. With such a certificate, you will be much more attractive to employers, many of whom would rather employ a TEFL-certified teacher without a degree than a university graduate without TEFL training and certification.

As you will see in the next chapter of this book, many different TEFL certificate courses are now available. If you do not have a degree, it is important to offset this disadvantage by obtaining the very best TEFL certification possible. In my opinion, this means that you should take a course leading to the Cambridge CELTA. Having the CELTA will increase your overseas job possibilities enormously. In parts of the world, the CELTA is actually accepted as a degree equivalent for the purposes of obtaining a work permit.

It is very important to note, however, that even having the CELTA will not gain you entry into the highest-paying TEFL job markets unless you also have a BA/BS degree. Because of government regulations, it is now absolutely impossible for anyone without a college degree to obtain legal work as a teacher in Arab countries or in Asian countries such as Taiwan, South Korea and Japan.

TEACHING WITH A DEGREE

Teaching With Only A Degree

If you have a BA/BS degree but do not have any specific TEFL/TESL training or qualifications, it should still be possible for you to find a job in many different parts of the world. For example, most of the organizations and schools which are listed in this book employ untrained teachers, sometimes on a regular basis and sometimes only in times of emergency. So do many of the schools which advertise on the "Jobs Offered" page of Dave's ESL Cafe (www.eslcafe.com) or on other Internet sites.

On the other hand, it is important to realize that looking for a TEFL position without having any specific training does have some serious drawbacks: it will be harder for you to find a good job, and it will be harder for you to do a good job.

If you are trying to decide whether you really need to take a TEFL-training course, I would strongly suggest that you bear the following points in mind:

- Reputable schools and organizations normally do not employ untrained teachers. So untrained teachers usually have to work for below-average employers; in other words, they usually end up in jobs which pay badly and provide comparatively poor working conditions.

  The North American professional association TESOL (Teachers of English to Speakers of Other Languages) states the problem clearly in its "Career Counsel" publication: "Pay scales tend to be low for those without training. If you are untrained and plan to search for a job, you will most likely find a position with low pay, no benefits, and many work hours."

- Even those overseas employers who are willing to employ untrained teachers would naturally rather hire trained ones. So if you apply for jobs with such employers, you probably will be competing against teachers who have training, and they are almost certain to win out every time.

- If you manage to obtain a job, it is going to be really hard for you to do the job well. Teaching EFL is by no means a simple job! To function effectively as a teacher, you need to have a good knowledge of English grammar, vocabulary and pronunciation. You also need to have good classroom management skills and to be able to make effective use of a range of specialized TEFL techniques and materials.

- Students overseas pay a lot of money for their EFL courses, and they naturally expect a lot from their teachers. If they do not get what they expect, they are generally very quick to criticize and to complain. It is one thing to be able to bluff your way into a TEFL job for which you are not qualified. It is quite another thing to be able to satisfy your students and keep your job!

Credentialed Teachers

If you already have a credential or experience as an elementary or high school teacher, it should not be too difficult for you to obtain a TEFL job overseas. However, you should still consider taking a specific training course, preferably one leading to a recognized TEFL certificate. There are several good reasons for taking such a course, particularly if you want to change to teaching adults rather than children:

• All of the best overseas TEFL employers now require specific EFL training and certification. As a professional teacher, you presumably want to find a good job overseas rather than to work for a low salary and for a less reputable employer.

• Even if you already have good classroom management skills, you are presumably not familiar with many of the very specific techniques and materials which are needed in the language teaching classroom.

• Unlike public school students in Canada and the USA, adult EFL students overseas generally pay very high fees for their English classes. As a result, they tend to be much more demanding and critical of their teachers. They expect their teachers to be able to explain, clearly and promptly, all aspects of English vocabulary, grammar and pronunciation. Any teacher who cannot do this will inevitably generate a lot of complaints, expressed either directly during classes or relayed to him/her via the employer.

BEING A NATIVE SPEAKER IS NOT ENOUGH

The Case For Specific Training

Many people assume that being an educated native speaker of English is enough to qualify someone to teach English to foreign students. Unfortunately, this is just not the case. There is a world of difference between being able to use your native language well and being able to clarify and teach it effectively and accurately to speakers of other languages.

If you think that you already have the language knowledge which it takes to be an effective and successful teacher of EFL, I suggest that you take a little time to check whether you really have the necessary depth of knowledge.

One way to do this is to observe a couple of intermediate or higher level classes in an EFL school for adult fee-paying students, and to see whether you would feel comfortable dealing with all of the language issues and questions which arise during the class. (Incidentally, I would not recommend that you observe ESL classes provided for immigrants. Since ESL courses for immigrants are provided free, the students who attend them are usually totally different in attitude, behavior and needs from the fee-paying students whom you will find in EFL classes overseas.)

An easier and quicker way to check your formal knowledge of English is to complete the "How Well Do You Know English?" test which you will find in Appendix 3. This will show you how well equipped you are to deal with the types of language questions which EFL students are likely to ask their teacher, and to which they expect accurate and prompt answers.

Training Yourself In TEFL Methodology

If you decide that you want to try teaching English overseas without first taking a specific TEFL-training course, you should certainly set aside some time to familiarize yourself with some basic features of language teaching methodology.

There are several good books which will provide you with an outline of TEFL methodology and help you to understand some basic language teaching skills and techniques.

I would strongly recommend that you read at least one of the following TEFL methodology books. All of them can be ordered through any good bookstore or from one of the EFL/ESL distributors listed in Appendix 2.

Teaching English Overseas

"Teach Yourself Teaching English" by David Riddell (Teach Yourself Books. ISBN0-340-78935-2)

"The Practice of English Language Teaching" by Jeremy Harmer (Longman. ISBN 0-582-04656-4)

"Teaching By Principles" by H. Douglas Brown (Prentice Hall Regents. ISBN 0-13-328220-1).

You should note that the book by Douglas Brown is significantly less practical in its approach than the others mentioned. However, it has the advantage of being written in American English, while the other books are in British English. You may also be able to get a copy of the book through any public or college library in North America.

You should also be able to learn a lot about TEFL techniques and activities from one of the better coursebooks produced for use in the EFL classroom. The most popular series of American English coursebooks is "New Interchange." The first book in the series is:

"New Interchange Intro" by Jack Richards (Cambridge University Press. ISBN 0-52-146744-6).

The most popular British English series of coursebooks is the "Headway"/"New Headway" series and the publishers have just started to produce American English versions of the books in the series. The first book in the series is:

"American Headway 1" by Liz & John Soars (Oxford University Press. ISBN 0-194-353753).

As you will realize, it is much easier to understand teaching skills and techniques if you can actually see them in action. So, if at all possible, you should try to find a way to observe some EFL/ESL classes, preferably given by teachers who are both trained and experienced. You should be able to arrange this by contacting private language schools or public ESL programs in your local area.

Learning More About English

Teaching any subject really well requires more than just methodological expertise. It also requires extensive knowledge of the subject which you are teaching. So, as was suggested above, you will certainly need

28

to work on improving your formal knowledge of English vocabulary, grammar and pronunciation. A relatively few hours spent in these ways will help you to make much more effective use of classroom teaching materials, and to answer many of the language questions which your students will ask you. It will also increase your chances of obtaining a TEFL job by making you appear better prepared and more knowledgeable in any job interviews!

There are many books which provide a good general introduction to language and linguistics; a good example is "An Introduction To Language" by Victoria Fromkin and Robert Rodman. Unfortunately, such books are essentially theoretical in their approach and they contain little that is of direct practical use to classroom teachers of English.

A better alternative is to buy one of the grammar books which have been produced for intermediate or advanced level foreign students of EFL. Although they are intended for use by students rather than teachers, the best of these books explain grammatical structures very clearly and simply. They also include practice exercises which will help you to understand and remember the structures which they cover. (If you buy one of them, be sure to check that it includes an answer key.) Perhaps the most useful book of this type is:

"Grammar In Use " by Raymond Murphy (Cambridge University Press. ISBN 0-521-34843-9).

There are also two books which are specifically designed to help EFL teachers to develop their knowledge of English grammar. One is:

"Explaining English Grammar" by George Yule (Oxford University Press. ISBN 0-19-437172-7).

The other is my own "A Grammar Development Course for American Teachers of EFL/ESL." This book evolved out of a series of assignments created for use by participants in Cambridge CELTA courses in North America, and all of the assignments have been widely praised by both TEFL professionals and CELTA course participants. The book is based around a series of practical tasks which will help you to develop a practical knowledge of some of the most important features of North American English grammar. Each task is accompanied by an answer key and detailed explanations.

You can find out more about the book and how to order it from the EI website (www.english-international.com).

When you are ready to start giving your first EFL lessons, I would recommend that you buy a copy of a good EFL grammar reference book and a good ESL dictionary. The grammar reference book that I personally find most useful is:

"Practical English Usage" by Michael Swan (Oxford University Press. ISBN 0-19-431197-X). Although this concentrates mainly on British English, it is still more useful than any of the American grammar books on the market.

This can be ordered from any good bookstore, from Amazon.com or from the EFL/ESL distributors listed in Appendix 2.

Chapter 3

Your TEFL Training Options

- **Available TEFL Training Programs**
- **How To Find A Suitable Program**
- **Choosing A TEFL Program**

INTRODUCTION

Throughout this book I suggest that, while it is still possible to teach EFL untrained, it is much better to think in terms of obtaining specific training and a formal TEFL qualification. This will help you to get a better job, and to do a better job. If you decide to take a TEFL training program, the first question to which you need to find an answer is "Which training program should I take?"

Many different training programs are now available in Canada and the USA, and many more are offered overseas. Unfortunately, as there is very little regulation of TEFL training courses anywhere in the world, the quality of programs varies enormously. A few programs provide excellent training while, at the other end of the spectrum, some are little more than scams.

The most popular training programs lead to some type of TEFL certificate. However, you should realize that "TEFL certificate" is just a generic term: virtually anyone can create and issue their own TEFL certificate. So when choosing a training course, it is essential that you find out to what extent the certificate which you will receive is recognized by employers.

31

In this chapter, I will outline the different kinds of programs which are available and will mention some of the advantages and drawbacks of each one. I will also suggest some questions which you should ask organizations when considering investing your time and money in one of their training programs.

However, I will start by quoting from an article about TEFL training options which I was commissioned to write by the "EL Gazette." The article originally appeared in the Gazette in 1998, but I believe that the points which I made in it are just as valid today.

"GETTING QUALIFIED AS AN EFL TEACHER

If you want to become an EFL teacher, start by taking a good TEFL certificate course. After nearly 30 years working in TEFL, I am convinced that this really is the best way to enter the field.

In as little as four weeks, a good certificate course can give you the practical hands-on training which you will need to get a worthwhile TEFL job and to carry out that job effectively. You can then gain classroom experience overseas and make sure you really enjoy this kind of teaching, before considering whether to invest time and money in a longer program, such as an MA TESOL.

What You Will Learn

Through a combination of methodology and language analysis seminars/workshops, supervised practice teaching, and feedback on practice lessons, a good TEFL certificate course will enable you to:

- learn and try out general teaching skills and specific TEFL techniques;
- make effective and creative use of TEFL materials;
- learn how to plan effective lessons which both you and your students will enjoy;
- improve your knowledge of English grammar, vocabulary and pronunciation, and your ability to clarify these to students;
- identify your strengths, and overcome your weaknesses, as a teacher.

A good certificate course will also:

- expose you to a variety of TEFL methodologies;
- help you to develop a personal teaching style;
- show you how to adjust your teaching to allow for different students' learning needs and preferences;
- motivate you and enable you to continue developing as a teacher after your initial training.

By the end of your course, you will have acquired the basic knowledge and skills which will then enable you to realize your full potential as a teacher. You will have gained confidence by having taught practice lessons with EFL classes. Also, you will have earned a certificate which will help you to secure a worthwhile teaching position overseas.

Choosing A TEFL Certificate Course

There are many TEFL certificate courses on the market, but they are not all equally effective or well regarded. Look for one which has a proven track record, is accredited to or validated by some external organization, and enjoys international recognition. Try to make sure that the course which you choose:

- is more than 100 hours long (and, if it is an intensive program, lasts no less than four weeks);
- includes at least six hours of supervised and evaluated practice teaching with classes of foreign students;
- takes account of a range of approaches (rather than restricting you to learning one methodology);
- has realistic objectives (because it is simply not possible for any short course to equip you for all types of teaching: General and Business English; adults and children; all levels, etc.).

The Cambridge CELTA

The program which I personally recommend over all others is the Cambridge CELTA - Certificate in English Language Teaching to Adults. (The course was previously known as the "RSA Cert," the "RSA/Cambridge CTEFLA" and the RSA/Cambridge CELTA.) The CELTA is undoubtedly the biggest and best known TEFL training program in the world, and it is probably also the most respected. Developed over many years and in consultation with literally thousands of EFL professionals and institutions, the CELTA program offers rigorous practical training based on sound TEFL principles. You can take a CELTA course, on an intensive or part-time basis, at any one of over 100 institutes worldwide."

AVAILABLE TEFL TRAINING PROGRAMS

MA TESOL Programs

Many US and Canadian universities offer MA TESOL programs, the best of which provide excellent practical TEFL training as well as a sound theoretical foundation in TESL/TEFL.

Unfortunately, however, many MA programs concentrate exclusively on theoretical issues rather than providing the kind of practical, hands-on training in classroom techniques and skills which is essential for new teachers. So, if you are considering taking an MA TESOL program, do not just assume that all such programs are equally effective. Instead, shop around until you find one that will provide you with appropriate classroom training, as well as with a good theoretical foundation.

Among the possible advantages of participating in an MA TESOL program are the following:

• Courses provide a good foundation in TESL/TEFL theory.

• Quality courses also provide supervised practice teaching.

• MA degrees are widely accepted by US employers.

• MA TESOL degrees are usually essential for non-classroom TEFL jobs (e.g., those involving program or materials design).

On the other hand, the possible disadvantages of at least some MA TESOL programs include the following:

- Programs are generally very expensive, with current costs ranging from a few thousand dollars to over $20,000.

- Most programs take at least 12-18 months to complete.

- Programs usually focus on TESL to immigrants in North America, rather than on TEFL to students overseas.

- Many courses provide little or no supervised hands-on training with classes of foreign students.

- Many MA TESOL degrees are not recognized as appropriate classroom teaching qualifications by overseas employers.

For a list of MA TESOL programs, you should consult the "Directory of Professional Preparation Programs in TESOL in the US & Canada," published by TESOL. Details of how to obtain the directory are given later in this chapter.

N. American University And College Certificate Programs

Many US and Canadian universities, colleges and community colleges now offer certificate programs in TESL or TESOL, usually on a part-time basis spread over several months. The main focus is almost always on the teaching of immigrants in North America, rather than on the teaching of EFL overseas. In general, the programs tend to be very theoretical, being based on lectures/seminars and the observation of ESL classes, with few programs providing opportunities for participants to undertake supervised practice teaching with real classes of foreign students.

The advantages of taking a university or college certificate program include the following:

- Most courses are comparatively inexpensive.

- University and college programs can usually be relied upon to provide a good theoretical introduction to TESL.

- Some (but by no means all) university/college certificate courses carry graduate credit recommendations.

Among the important disadvantages of most, but not all, of these certificate programs are the following:

• Programs usually focus on TESL to immigrants in Canada or the USA, rather than on TEFL to foreign students overseas.

• There is usually no hands-on training with foreign students.

• Most university or college TEFL/TESL certificates are not recognized by the better employers overseas.

Recognized Certificate Programs In N. America

There are only two TEFL certificate programs which are universally respected throughout the TEFL world, and which are recognized and accepted by virtually all overseas employers. These are the Cambridge CELTA and the Trinity College Certificate in TESOL. As Susan Griffith puts it in her "Teaching English Abroad" book: "Anyone with the Cambridge/RSA or Trinity Certificate is in a much stronger position to get a job in any country where English is widely taught."

Both certificates require participation in a face-to-face training program at an approved center, and they cannot be completed via any form of distance learning. This is because both programs place great emphasis on the need for supervised practice teaching.

At present, only the Cambridge CELTA is available in the USA and Canada, and so North Americans who want to obtain the Trinity Certificate will have to travel overseas to take a course. (Both programs are available at a range of centers elsewhere in the world, and I will discuss later in this chapter the advisability of participating in a CELTA or Trinity College course outside of North America.)

The Cambridge CELTA

The CELTA, formerly known as the "RSA Certificate" and the "RSA/Cambridge CTEFLA," is regarded throughout the English teaching world as being the best and most useful of all TEFL certificates. This is partly because it is also the biggest TEFL training and certification program worldwide, with about 8000 teachers a year taking CELTA courses. (The fact that Cambridge University has had an excellent reputation for many years also helps, of course.)

Although the CELTA is administered from Cambridge in England, the qualification is very much an international (rather than a British) one. The current version of the program was developed in 1996-97 after several years of detailed consultation between Cambridge and literally thousands of employers, teachers, academics and other TEFL professionals all around the world.

You can currently take a CELTA at any one of twelve approved training centers in the USA and Canada, and at well over a hundred centers in other countries. For contact details, see Appendix 1.

The syllabus and the evaluation criteria are standardized, and all CELTA centers have to meet very tough quality control regulations established and monitored by Cambridge. Every center is required to provide supervised and evaluated practice teaching with classes of adult foreign students (at different levels), together with expert feedback on these practice lessons. All courses also include at least eight hours' observation of EFL classes given by trained and experienced teachers.

It should be noted that, while ensuring that all centers meet the program's rigorous minimum standards, Cambridge allows each center a fair degree of autonomy in designing its courses to reflect local needs and conditions. The result is that individual CELTA courses can vary quite significantly in terms of content, schedule, cost, staffing, amount of job assistance provided, etc. It is particularly important to note that, since the program is truly international in nature, CELTA courses in Canada and the USA provide training in the teaching of North American English using North American coursebooks and materials.

To give you an idea of how widely the CELTA is respected and recognized, here are just a few comments on the program taken from some major TEFL job guides:

- "The most popular course for first-time teachers is the RSA/ Cambridge CELTA" (Nuala O'Sullivan in "Teaching English in South-East Asia").

- "Anyone with the RSA/Cambridge Certificate is in a very strong position to get a job in any country where English is widely taught" (Susan Griffith in "Teaching English Overseas").

- "The most widely recognized and respected basic TEFL qualification" ("ELT Guide").

- "Of the numerous TEFL certificate programs available, the most widely recognized is the RSA/Cambridge CELTA" (TESOL's "Career Counsel 1998-1999").

Advantages And Disadvantages Of The CELTA

The CELTA program provides course participants with a long list of major benefits and very few disadvantages.

Among the many important advantages of the Cambridge CELTA program are the following:

- Every CELTA center and program undergoes a rigorous annual approval process.

- A Cambridge-appointed assessor visits every single course which is offered.

- Courses provide expert instruction in methodology and language analysis given by experienced, qualified and trained trainers.

- Courses provide training in a non-dogmatic communicative approach, which is based on modern methodologies, proven classroom techniques, and up-to-date research. The approach can be adapted to meet the needs of students in many different contexts.

- Each participant is provided with six hours of supervised and evaluated practice teaching with real classes of foreign students. (Some centers also provide unevaluated practice teaching.)

- Evaluation is carried out using an internationally-agreed grading system, and only participants who attain a good standard of teaching are awarded the certificate. This is extremely important from an employer's point of view, as it basically guarantees that anyone who has gained the CELTA is an effective classroom teacher. (It should be noted that, since centers are required to screen all applications with great care, well over 90% of CELTA program participants worldwide pass their course and obtain the certificate.)

• Some CELTA courses carry a graduate credit recommendation.

I personally have taught on more than a hundred Cambridge TEFL certificate courses. From 1993 until 1998, I was also the CELTA Joint Chief Assessor for North America, responsible for monitoring standards in all Cambridge-approved centers. In my opinion, all of the CELTA programs currently offered in the USA and Canada operate to high educational and ethical standards.

Based on my experience, I believe that CELTA courses have only three possibly significant disadvantages:

• Because centers are required to operate with a high trainer:trainee ratio, their courses are normally somewhat more expensive than those offered by independent institutes. (I believe that the extra amount of personal attention which each participant receives is well worth the extra cost, but some people would not agree with this view.)

• Courses usually operate on a 4-week intensive basis and most centers do not offer part-time courses. This means that, in common with all other intensive training courses, people cannot hold down other employment during the period of their training.

• Intensive CELTA courses are very demanding and participants have to be prepared to put the rest of their lives on hold for the four weeks of their course. In addition to class hours, participants can expect to spend three hours each evening on lesson planning and the whole of one day each weekend on other assignments.

CELTA And Trinity Courses Overseas

Americans and Canadians can obtain the Cambridge CELTA or the Trinity College TESOL Certificate by taking an approved course in any country where the programs are offered. (CELTA courses are offered in most areas of the world, except Latin America; most Trinity courses take place in Europe, but some exist in other areas.) You should note that you will receive exactly the same certificate wherever you take a course, and that employers normally will accept the certificate irrespective of where the training took place.

The only major advantage which you may gain from taking a Cambridge or Trinity College course overseas rather than a CELTA course in North America is that of lower fees. (I say "may" because courses in countries such as Japan can be even more expensive than those in North America.) If you follow a course in a less-developed country such as Egypt or Thailand, the total cost of your airfare/accommodation/tuition package may be little more than just the tuition fee for a similar course in the USA.

If your sole employment aim is to teach in one particular country, you may gain some additional advantages from doing your training there. For example, you will gain experience teaching classes of students from the country. Also, the training center may have links with local schools; or you may be able to check out local employers even during your course. However, you should not assume that all training centers provide job placement assistance. You should also realize that taking a course in a particular country will not enable you to circumvent local work permit regulations; so, for example, Americans and Canadians who train in a European Union country will still find it virtually impossible to obtain work in that country.

Having observed or worked on TEFL courses in several countries, I would give the following five pieces of advice to any Americans and Canadians thinking of taking a Cambridge or Trinity course overseas:

1 Before enrolling, ask the center what job possibilities exist for you in the local area and exactly how much job placement assistance you will receive. Also, ask whether the center will give you any job placement help if and when you want to teach in another country.

2 Find out whether the course caters for different varieties of English. I would strongly recommend any North American against taking a course which deals exclusively or mainly with the analysis and teaching of, for example, British English. Both CELTA and Trinity College programs are very tough; you do not want to make life even tougher for yourself by taking a course in what will sometimes seem to you like a totally foreign language!

3 If you are from the USA, make sure that the trainers have some experience with training Americans. Educational approaches and assumptions vary enormously between, for example, the USA and the UK. I have known many Americans who did British-based TEFL courses in Europe and elsewhere. In many cases, they felt that they were at a real disadvantage because they and their trainers came from very different educational (and cultural) backgrounds.

4 Unless you are a very seasoned traveler, avoid taking a course in any country where the culture, language and climate will be alien to you. You certainly do not want to have to deal with culture shock as well as with a very tough training course.

5 If you are going to be taking an intensive course, do not expect to see much of the local country during the course. You simply will not have time to do so - these courses really are intensive!

Independent Certificate Programs In N. America

In the past few years, several US and Canadian institutes have created their own independent TEFL certificate programs, which are offered in a number of North American cities and sometimes also overseas. These programs, which typically last three or four weeks, almost always combine lectures and workshops with some hours of supervised practice teaching.

Unfortunately, as there is no agreed system for monitoring and regulating independent TEFL certificate programs in North America, the standard of training which is provided by these centers varies enormously, as does the international validity of the certification which they offer.

If you are considering an independent TEFL certificate program, it is very important to avoid taking at face value all of the claims which they make in their (often very slick and very well-crafted) publicity materials. Instead, you should research the program carefully, and try to obtain independent verification of any claims which are made. For example, contact some local language schools and/or university TESL departments to find out their views on the validity of the program.

In the case of any programs offered in California, you should check that they hold a current license from the state's Bureau for Private Postsecondary and Vocational Education. You can contact the BPPVE by phone at (916) 327-8900.

Since some institutes have been known to engage in questionable business practices, I would also suggest that you check out each institute's record with the local branch of the Better Business Bureau.

The possible advantages of participating in an independent TEFL certificate program include the following:

• Courses usually cost less than more recognized programs.

• Most programs include some practical hands-on training.

• Courses are usually very easy to enter and to complete.

• Some TEFL employers accept the certificates.

On a more negative note, you may find that programs suffer from some or all of the following disadvantages:

• Courses may be taught by unqualified staff with little experience.

• Training is often in outdated and restrictive methods.

• Practice teaching may involve teaching peers rather than actual foreign students, and some or all of it may be unsupervised.

• Independent training centers have been known to close with little or no warning, leaving their graduates with worthless certificates.

• Many TEFL employers (including most of the better ones) do not recognize some or all independent certificates.

• To obtain an overseas job, you will often have to travel to the foreign country (at your expense) to give a demonstration lesson.

• Courses rarely if ever carry graduate credits.

"In-House" Training Programs

Several language school groups offer courses to train teachers to work in their schools. Such courses usually last 1-2 weeks, and they provide practical training in the specific method used in that group's schools.

The main advantages of in-house courses are clear:

- Courses are short and often inexpensive (or even free).
- Training may lead to jobs in one of the chain's schools.

However, most TEFL professionals would probably agree that the disadvantages of in-house training courses far outweigh the benefits which they offer. The major disadvantages include:

- Programs often deal with only one specific teaching method, which may be regarded by other employers as being outdated and restrictive.
- Courses are usually too short to permit really effective training.
- Training is not recognized by other TEFL/TESL employers.
- You will not normally receive any credits if you later decide to enter an MA TESOL program.

Distance Learning TEFL Programs

Many distance learning TEFL programs are available, conducted by correspondence or on-line, and their main attractions are obvious: convenience and low cost. While some of these programs offer quality instruction and training, some are totally worthless. As Kristen Schwartz writes in TESOL's "Career Counsel" publication, "there are fly-by-night schools that offer courses over the Internet, take your money, and then disappear without awarding your TEFL certificate."

Even some of the more reputable distance learning programs suffer from one disadvantage: the certification which they provide may not be recognized by some major TEFL employers.

If you opt to take a distance TEFL course, look for one which lasts at least 100 hours and preferably, unless you have previous teaching experience, one that offers the option of carrying out six hours of practice teaching. This teaching usually will involve your arranging classes, privately or at a local institute, and video-taping lessons to send in for critiquing. Any TEFL certificate which does not include practice teaching will be regarded by some employers as being only an introductory certificate and this will limit your employment prospects.

So, in job placement terms, a distance learning course that lasts less than 100 hours and does not include evaluated practice teaching will only help you to compete against untrained teachers; it will not help you to compete successfully with teachers who have completed one of the better face-to-face training courses.

TEFL Training Workshops And Short Courses

Some US and Canadian organizations offer short training workshops or courses, most of which take a week or less to complete, and several of these organizations issue participants with a "TEFL certificate." To the best of my knowledge, no reputable TEFL employer anywhere recognizes such certificates. This is hardly surprising: As Susan Griffith points out in her "Teaching English Abroad" book, "It would be unreasonable to expect a weekend or five-day course to equip anyone to teach."

So, in job placement terms, the only value of workshops and short courses is that they may help you to compete more successfully for jobs with employers who generally recruit untrained teachers.

HOW TO FIND A SUITABLE PROGRAM

To find out about North American university MA TESOL and TEFL/ TESL certification programs, get ahold of a copy of the "Directory of Professional Preparation Programs in TESOL in the US and Canada." Published by the professional association TESOL, this gives details of over 400 programs offered in more than 200 institutions. You can get more information on the directory, and can order a copy, by contacting: TESOL, 700 S. Washington Street, Suite 200, Alexandria, VA 22314, USA. The phone number is (703) 836-0774. The website address is: www.tesol.org.

For information on TEFL/TESL training programs offered by community colleges, you need to contact individual colleges.

Appendix 1 of this book includes a list of North American centers which offer CELTA and independent TEFL certificate courses. You will find that virtually all of the reputable programs are also listed in the TESOL association's "Career Counsel" booklet, which you can order from TESOL in Alexandria.

Many of the certificate programs which operate in North America advertise in "Transitions Abroad" magazine. You should be able to buy a copy at major newsstands, or to consult a copy in major public libraries, university career centers, etc. The magazine also contains many useful articles on traveling and living abroad.

For a fairly comprehensive list of TEFL training courses in other countries, you should look in "The ELT Guide," which can be purchased from TESOL in Alexandria. You could also look in the most recent edition of Susan Griffith's book "Teaching English Abroad." You can buy or order this from any good bookstore. It is published by Vacation Work and distributed by Peterson's Guides.

You can obtain an up-to-date list of Cambridge CELTA centers, in North America and elsewhere, from: Cambridge ELT, University of Cambridge, 1 Hills Road, Cambridge, CB1 2EU, England. A full list is also carried on the Cambridge website, which you can find at: www.cambridge-efl.org.

For information on Trinity College TESOL Certificate courses, contact: Trinity College, 16 Park Crescent, London, W1N 4AP, England. The e-mail address is: info@trinitycollege.co.uk and the web site address is: www.trinitycollege.co.uk.

CHOOSING AN ON-SITE TEFL PROGRAM

Evaluating TEFL Training Programs

As I have tried to stress above, it is extremely important not to make the mistake of thinking that all TEFL programs are equal. It is an unfortunate fact that not all training courses are good; and that not even all of the good ones will necessarily meet your particular needs. You also need to bear in mind that your choice of training course will greatly influence not only your initial teaching ability and job possibilities, but also your later career and further education options. So you need to be ready to devote some time to researching in considerable depth any program which you are considering taking.

I hope that my comments earlier in this chapter will help you to choose the training course which is most appropriate for you. You can also obtain useful advice from some of the organizations and publications mentioned above in the section on "Finding TEFL Courses."

If you have Internet access, you should also check out postings on Teacher Training page of Dave's ESL Cafe (www.eslcafe.com). These postings often include useful comments by graduates of the various programs, as well as by TEFL employers and by training centers. However, take what you read with a grain of salt! The occasional negative comment from a graduate of any particular program may say more about the person making the posting than about the program concerned. Also, remember that complimentary postings about particular programs may actually be posted by people working for or paid by those same programs.

A Checklist Of Possible Questions

In case you feel overwhelmed by all of the factors involved in evaluating different courses, I have included below a detailed list of what I feel are relevant questions. I would strongly suggest that you ask the various training centers as many of the questions as you feel are important to you. (I have not included "obvious" questions about course dates, duration, tuition, etc.)

Incidentally, this does not mean that you have to spend hours on the phone. Start by getting and carefully reading a copy of the program's brochure or catalog. That should provide answers to many or most of the questions which I have suggested. Then call the center on the phone and ask any questions to which you have not yet been able to find a satisfactory answer.

In my view, you should be extremely wary of any center which is unable or reluctant to answer any of these questions. Be particularly wary of centers which are not prepared to spend time on the phone with you: if they will not give you time when they are trying to persuade you to enroll, how much time will they give you once they have received your money?

The Questions

Here are twenty questions which I think you should ask about any on-site TEFL program that you are seriously considering. Where appropriate, I have commented on some of the questions.

* Who issues the certificate which you will receive?
  (Employers generally prefer certificates which are issued or validated by external bodies, such as colleges or universities.)

* How widely is the certificate known and recognized overseas?
  (Ask to see advertisements or letters which specifically mention the certificate which you will receive at the end of your training.)

* Which professional body approves and monitors the program?
  (If you want to be sure of receiving quality training, look for a program which is approved by or accredited with a university or some other external body.)

* Does an outside assessor visit the program? If so, how often?
  (Quality programs such as the CELTA or the Trinity College TESOL are rigorously monitored, with every month's course being visited by an assessor or inspector who is appointed by an external validating body.)

* How long has the center been offering training course?
  (A totally new program is unlikely to be known to employers.)

* If you have to cancel or drop your course, will you receive a full or partial refund of your fees?
  (Most reputable centers should give a more or less full refund if you withdraw at any time before the course start date. They will also give a pro rata refund if you drop during the course.)

* What are the minimum qualifications required of all trainers?
  (Avoid any program where the trainers do not have at least five

years of TEFL experience and do not have either an MA TESOL
or a recognized Diploma in TEFL.)

- What is the maximum size of each course?
  (Some programs accept as many people as choose to apply.
  Courses with more than 15-18 participants are unlikely to
  provide effective training.)

- What is the ratio of full-time trainers to course participants?
  (You are unlikely to receive enough individualized guidance if the
  ratio is worse than 1:6.)

- How long is the course in clock hours, excluding all breaks for
  coffee, lunch, etc.?
  (Employers do not usually recognize courses of fewer than 100
  clock hours. Some programs inflate the number of course hours
  by including breaks, time spent on homework tasks, etc.)

- What pre-course materials and assignments will be provided to
  help you to prepare for your course?
  (The better programs will require you to carry out some pre-
  course tasks, usually in the area of language analysis.)

- How many course hours are devoted to the analysis of English
  grammar, vocabulary and pronunciation?
  (I would suggest that an absolute minimum of 12 hours should be
  spent on these important areas. That should be in addition to any
  pre-course or homework assignments which you are required to
  complete.)

- How many hours of supervised and evaluated practice teaching
  will you have with classes of foreign students?
  (The internationally recognized standard is six hours of supervised and evaluated solo teaching. This should be in addition to
  any team-teaching which may take place. All supervised practice
  lessons should be followed by oral and written feedback from a
  trainer.)

- Will this practice teaching include a full range of lesson types,
  including lessons dealing with grammar and vocabulary?
  (You should have more than one opportunity to teach at least the

following lesson types: free speaking; grammar clarification and practice; vocabulary clarification and practice; reading skills; and listening skills. You should also carry out practice teaching with at least two different levels of classes; for example, Elementary and Intermediate.)

* How many hours will you spend observing EFL classes given by trained teachers?
  (You can learn a great deal from observing good teachers. Most of the better courses arrange for you to observe 6-8 hours of lessons given by trained, experienced teachers.)

* What access will you have to photocopiers, computers and the Internet during the course?
  (You will need access to photocopiers when you are preparing your practice lessons. You will need computer and Internet access when carrying out your job search.)

* What job placement assistance is given during the course?
  (You cannot expect training centers to arrange a job for you. However, you should expect to receive more help than just a couple of lectures about finding jobs. Look for a program which provides good job search resources and some individualized job placement guidance.)

* Does this assistance continue after the course? If so, for how long?
  (The better programs will allow you access to their job search and job guidance resources after your course has ended. For example, they will send you employers` addresses and will comment on job offers which you receive. This type of assistance should be provided free for at least one year after your course.)

* What are the qualifications and experience of the people who provide job placement assistance?
  (Job placement guidance is worthless unless it is provided by experienced TEFL professionals. Look for a program where job guidance is provided by TEFL trainers with extensive overseas experience.)

* Will you receive a graduate credit recommendation for the

course? If so, how many semester hours will this cover? (If you decide to make a career in TEFL, you will almost certainly need to obtain a Masters degree at some point. Some TEFL certificate programs carry an MA TESOL credit recommendation of six semester hours.)

Applying The Above Criteria To Distance Programs

It would be unfair to apply the above criteria to most distance TEFL programs. Such programs generally are much less expensive than on-site certificate programs and therefore you cannot really expect them to offer all of the same features!

If you are thinking of taking a distance TEFL course, here are some points you should:

- If the course lasts less than 100 hours, does it clearly label itself as being an "introductory" course or does it try to claim that it offers a full TEFL certificate?

- Does the course include a practice teaching option? (The best employers recognize only courses that include six hours of evaluated practice teaching.)

- Is the course run by a reputable organization that has been involved in TEFL training for several years?

- Who will evaluate your assignments and act as your tutor during the course? Can you be sure of having the same tutor throughout your course? What TEFL experience and qualifications does this person have?
  (TEFL training needs to be very personalized and so you want to have one tutor with whom you can build a relationship. It is very important that this person have the appropriate qualifications and experience.)

Chapter 4

An Overview Of The Job Market

- **Introduction**
- **Region-By-Region Overview**

INTRODUCTION

One of the great advantages of TEFL over other types of overseas work is that there are always numerous job opportunities in many different regions of the world. So it usually is not difficult to find a job in the region or the type of country which most appeals to you.

As a North American, you can expect to find TEFL job opportunities in most areas of the world: Asia, Latin America, Central and Eastern Europe, North Africa and the Mid East. Later in this chapter, you will find an overview of the current TEFL job market in these and other areas. Also, in Appendix 5, you will find contact details for employers in the various regions.

Unfortunately, the picture is not all rosy and there are regions and countries where it is very difficult to find work, usually because of prevailing political and/or economic factors. At present, the regions where it is particularly difficult for Canadian and US teachers to find work are: other English-speaking countries; Western Europe; the Indian subcontinent; and sub-Saharan Africa. More information on the TEFL employment situation in these areas is given in the region-by-region overview which follows.

ENGLISH-SPEAKING COUNTRIES

The more affluent English-speaking countries such as Australia and New Zealand are very reluctant to grant work permits to EFL teachers from other countries. This is because they feel that their TEFL employment needs can be met from within their own populations, and they want to protect their own citizens from having to compete for jobs with foreign workers. A similar situation faces teachers from those countries who want to find jobs in Canada and the USA.

In some other English-speaking countries, the employment situation for North Americans is also limited by other factors. For example, Britain and Ireland are both members of the European Union and so they are subject to the very stringent restrictions which the EU places on the employment of non-EU citizens. Elsewhere, economically less-developed countries in the Indian subcontinent, sub-Saharan Africa and the West Indies have very small or nonexistent EFL markets; in addition, they cannot afford to pay the salaries or provide the working conditions which North American teachers expect or require.

This is not to say that it is totally impossible for North Americans to work in other English-speaking countries. For example, teachers with advanced qualifications or extensive teaching experience may be able to find positions in universities or in public schools in some of the more affluent countries. In less-developed countries, such teachers may be able to find employment through various educational aid programs sponsored by the Canadian or US governments. Also, some North American citizens may be able to claim citizenship of or residence rights in other English-speaking countries through marriage or because they have parents from those countries.

AFRICA: NORTH

The TEFL Market

Because of political factors, the market is currently very small, being limited to Morocco, Tunisia and Egypt. Teachers normally must have a BA/BS degree, and the better jobs require a TEFL certificate and/or previous TEFL experience.

Arranging Jobs and Work Permits

Some jobs can be obtained in advance through organizations such as the US-based Amideast. However, most jobs can only be obtained from inside the countries. Employers will normally obtain the necessary work permits, provided that the teacher has a BA/BS degree.

Employment Conditions

Contracts start at any time of the year and generally last 12 months, extendable by mutual consent. Locally-obtained jobs may be on a fixed contract basis or may involve working on a month-to-month basis.

A typical schedule requires teachers to work 20-25 hours per week, Sunday through Thursday, and to teach both morning and evening classes. One year contracts usually include 4-6 weeks of paid vacation. While salaries allow a comfortable lifestyle, they rarely permit savings of more than perhaps $200-$300 a month.

Employers do not pay airfare for teachers who are recruited locally. Most employers help teachers to arrange housing, but very few pay for the cost of this housing.

AFRICA: SUB-SAHARAN

The TEFL Market

There are very few TEFL jobs in the region: public schools cannot afford foreign teachers, and few private language schools exist. A small number of relatively good jobs exist in US-sponsored institutes, but there is a tremendous amount of competition for these jobs. To be successful, applicants normally need to have an MA TESOL and previous teaching experience.

Other jobs are extremely difficult to find, even if you are prepared to travel to the country concerned. For teachers who are really determined to travel to Africa to find work, the best countries to try are currently Mozambique and Kenya.

For most new teachers, the only practicable way to find a TEFL job in the area is through aid programs run by religious groups or by organizations such as the Peace Corps.

Employment Conditions

The type of positions which new teachers are likely to obtain usually offer extremely poor salaries and working conditions. Living conditions can also be very difficult.

ASIA

The TEFL Market

There are almost limitless opportunities for both trained and untrained teachers in Japan, South Korea, Taiwan, China, Thailand and Indonesia, and there is a rapidly expanding market in Vietnam. There are much more limited opportunities in Laos, Cambodia, Singapore and Malaysia. Most jobs are in private language schools and may involve teaching both adults and younger learners, but teachers with a recognized TEFL certificate may also find employment in public or private colleges or universities. In Taiwan and Korea, many positions involve teaching children as young as five years of age.

Except for people working through church groups or aid organizations, new teachers will find it virtually impossible to obtain jobs in other countries, including: Bangladesh, Brunei, Burma, India, Nepal, Pakistan, the Philippines and Sri Lanka.

Arranging Jobs and Work Permits

Trained teachers should have no difficulty in arranging good jobs from North America. As is normally required by law, most employers arrange work permits before the teacher's departure from North America. However, permits are sometimes arranged by the employer after the teacher has arrived in the overseas country.

Untrained teachers or those with TEFL certificates which are not internationally recognized will sometimes be able to arrange jobs from North America. This is particularly true if they are heading to Korea or China, or if they are applying through the JET Program for jobs in Japan. However, in most cases, teachers who do not hold a recognized TEFL certificate will find it necessary to travel to the overseas country to obtain work. If they are successful, their employers will normally be able to arrange the required permits and visas once the teachers have started work.

Japan, Korea and Taiwan now require that all foreign teachers hold a BS or BA degree, and it is absolutely impossible to work legally in these countries without such a degree. Some other countries, such as Thailand and China, are currently considering introducing similar restrictions.

Employment Conditions

Contracts are normally available at any time of the year and they are generally for one year.

A typical contract in most countries in the region involves teaching five days and 20-25 hours per week, and it also provides for 4-6 weeks of paid annual vacation. However, teachers in the higher paying countries (Japan, Korea and Taiwan) frequently have to teach six days and 30-35 hours per week, and may receive only 1-2 weeks of paid annual vacation.

Teachers who arrange jobs in advance in China, Japan and Korea will usually have their airfare paid by the employer; in some cases, the employer will expect the teacher to buy the ticket but will reimburse him/her on arrival in the overseas country.

Employers normally provide housing (usually free) to teachers who prearrange jobs from North America.

Salaries vary greatly throughout the region but they are always high enough to allow a comfortable lifestyle. Teachers in the highest paying countries (Korea, Taiwan and Japan) work relatively long hours but they can save $600-$1000 a month or even more. In Indonesia, Singapore, Thailand and Vietnam, teachers work fewer hours and shorter weeks, but they also save less. However, teachers in these countries often devote some of their leisure time to teaching extra lessons and this can enable them to save $400-$600 or more a month. In most other countries in the region, salaries for new teachers do not permit significant savings.

EUROPE: EU COUNTRIES

The TEFL Market

There are large numbers of jobs in language schools throughout most of Western Europe, but it is virtually impossible for Americans and Canadians to obtain a work permit and residence visa, unless they hold an EU passport. (This does not prevent thousands of North Americans from working illegally in Europe, often for many years.)

Virtually all reputable employers require teachers to have a TEFL certificate. The most useful certificates are the Cambridge CELTA and the Trinity College TESOL Certificate.

Work Permit Restrictions

While it is generally extremely difficult for non-EU citizens to obtain work permits, it is sometimes possible. In some countries, you may be eligible for a work permit if you first obtain a job; this is sometimes possible in Greece, Germany, Finland and Italy. In the other countries, where normal work permits are very rarely issued to non-EU citizens, it is sometimes possible for North Americans to apply for a work permit as an "independent worker." However, obtaining this kind of permit is a complicated and often expensive process, which usually involves the hiring of an immigration lawyer. As the rules governing "independent worker" status tend to change frequently, you should contact the relevant consulate to find out the current situation.

If you are really desperate to work in an EU country, you might try contacting the relevant consulate to ask about student visas. In some cases, foreigners who are enrolled in an approved language or other study program in a country may be able to obtain a special student/ work visa which will allow them to work at least part-time to finance their studies. If you have a parent or grandparent from the country, you should also ask whether you are eligible for citizenship of the country.

Pre-Arranging Jobs

Even if you have EU citizenship, it is rarely possible to arrange a TEFL job in advance from North America. In virtually all cases, the only way to get a job is to go to the country and approach schools on the spot.

If you have the CELTA or the Trinity TESOL Certificate, you might be able to arrange a job in advance through one of the major school chains or recruitment agencies based in England. However, these chains and agencies almost always require applicants to travel to the UK at their own expense for an interview. It should also be noted that most of these employers do not recognize independent North American TEFL certificates; some of them do not even recognize MA TESOL degrees.

Employment Conditions

Most jobs start in September/October, but some are also available in January. Contracts normally last 9-12 months. Illegal jobs normally involve working on a month-by-month basis.

Jobs generally involve 20-25 hours of teaching per week, Monday through Friday. Year contracts usually include 4-6 weeks of paid vacation. Base salaries are rarely high enough to permit savings of more than $200 a month.

Teachers recruited via England through organizations such as International House are often paid the roundtrip airfare from London to the country of work, and they may also receive (nonfinancial) assistance with arranging housing. Other teachers almost always have to arrange and pay their own airfare and accommodations.

EUROPE: NON-EU COUNTRIES

The TEFL Market

Although a few Western European countries are still not EU members, almost all TEFL job opportunities for North Americans are in the former Eastern bloc countries of Central and Eastern Europe. So, for example, there are currently almost unlimited numbers of jobs for both trained and untrained teachers in Poland and the Czech Republic. A significant number of jobs are also available in Hungary and Russia, while more limited opportunities exist in most of the other countries in the region.

Arranging Jobs and Work Permits

Teachers who have a recognized TEFL certificate such as the CELTA should find it relatively easy to arrange jobs in advance from North America by replying to ads on the Internet or by contacting specific schools or agencies. Many or most of the best jobs are with British-based organizations, but these often require that applicants travel to the UK (at their own expense) for an interview.

Teachers who do not have a TEFL certificate, or who have one which is not widely recognized, can normally obtain jobs only by traveling to the country concerned.

Teachers who obtain jobs should have no problems with obtaining the necessary work permits and visas.

Employment Conditions

At present, employment (and living) conditions for foreign teachers are generally best in Poland, Hungary, the Czech Republic, Russia, Slovakia, Slovenia, Lithuania and Estonia.

Working conditions in countries such as Albania, Romania and Bulgaria tend to be less good, and living conditions can be extremely primitive. For most teachers, the best way to obtain reasonable living and working conditions in these countries is through participation in programs operated by aid organizations such as the Peace Corps and the SOROS Foundation.

Most prearranged contracts start in September/October or in January and are for 9-12 months. Jobs which are arranged locally can be on a month-by-month basis, but the best time to find work is still either September/October or January. In Poland, Hungary and the Czech Republic, summer work is sometimes available; this usually involves teaching EFL to children at summer camps.

Most jobs involve 20-25 hours of teaching per week, Monday through Friday, but there are a few employers who require teachers to work six days a week. Year contracts usually include at least 4 weeks of paid vacation. Salaries are rarely high enough to permit savings of more than $200 a month, unless teachers supplement them with income from private lessons.

Except for organizations such as the Peace Corps and the SOROS Foundation, employers rarely pay airfares. In contrast, housing is often provided and paid by the employer. As housing in most Central and Eastern European capitals is relatively expensive, teachers who want to work in cities such as Prague and Budapest may have to share very small apartments or to live with local families. Housing in smaller cities is much less of a problem, but it is still of poor quality by North American standards.

LATIN AMERICA

The TEFL Market

Latin America is a really enormous TEFL market, with tens of thousands of jobs available every year in language schools, binational centers and universities. In some countries, teachers can also find work teaching EFL to younger learners in private elementary and high schools. Jobs vary greatly in quality from country to country, and even within individual countries. Many of the positions are open to unqualified teachers, but most of the better employers now recruit only expatriate teachers who have a BA/BS degree and/or a TEFL certificate.

Mexico is the easiest market in which to find a job, even for teachers

· who have no formal qualifications or training. It is probably also the easiest country for Americans and Canadians to adapt to. Central America is another area where it is generally easy to find work, but jobs there offer poor working conditions and only survival salaries. Further south, the largest TEFL markets are in Brazil and Argentina, followed by Colombia and Ecuador; all of these countries offer comparatively good working conditions. A much smaller number of jobs are available in Venezuela, Peru, Chile, Bolivia and Uruguay.

Arranging Jobs and Work Permits

In most countries, there are some jobs which can be prearranged from North America, by responding to ads on the Internet or by contacting schools directly. However, many employers will only offer contracts to applicants who are willing to travel to the country for an interview. This is particularly likely to happen in the case of untrained teachers or of teachers who have never lived overseas.

Work permit regulations tend to be very relaxed, and teachers who obtain jobs should have no problems with obtaining the necessary work permits and visas.

Employment Conditions

Prearranged contracts start at any time of the year, although very few jobs in South America start between November and February. Most contracts are for one year, renewable by mutual consent. In the case of employers who recruit locally, teachers may be offered work on a month-by-month basis.

Jobs generally involve 20-25 hours of teaching per week, Monday through Friday. One year contracts usually include 4-6 weeks of paid vacation. Except in the case of Argentina, salaries are rarely high enough to permit savings of more than $200 a month, unless teachers supplement them with income from private lessons.

It should be noted that employers in Latin America rarely pay airfares for new teachers. Also, although most schools will help new arrivals to find suitable accommodations, they do not usually pay the cost of this housing.

THE MID EAST & TURKEY

The TEFL Market

Because of political factors, the TEFL market in the Mid East is now much smaller than it was 20 or 30 years ago. A few jobs exist in Syria and Jordan, but most opportunities in the region are in the countries of the Arabian Gulf: Saudi Arabia, Kuwait and the UAE (United Arab Emirates). There are generally more positions for men than for women, and employers tend to prefer applicants who are over 25 years of age. A BA/BS degree is essential, and most jobs require at least a TEFL certificate.

Turkey has a very large number of private language schools, and it is easy for both trained and untrained teachers to find jobs. However, teachers should carry out their job hunt with caution, because some schools treat their employees extremely badly. The largest numbers of jobs (and many of the best ones) are in Istanbul and Ankara, but it is now possible to find jobs in almost every town in the country. Many foreigners find that life is more relaxed and enjoyable in towns such as Izmir than in the bigger cities.

Arranging Jobs and Work Permits

For legal reasons, most jobs in the Mid East have to be arranged in advance. They can be obtained by replying to ads on the Internet or in the TESOL Placement Bulletin, or by contacting recruitment agencies which specialize in Mid East jobs.

Once a teacher has signed a formal employment contract, the employer will start to arrange the necessary work permits and visas. As a rule, the teacher cannot travel to the country until all of the bureaucratic procedures have been completed, which may take several weeks. If the process happens to coincide with the Islamic holy month of Ramadan, it may take even longer.

Trained teachers should be able to prearrange jobs in Turkey, while untrained teachers will usually have to travel there to obtain work. Once work has been obtained, the employer will arrange the necessary permits and visas.

Employment Conditions

Contracts start at any time of the year and are generally for one year. An exception is Saudi Arabia, where contracts for as little as four months are sometimes available. Teachers who find work locally in Turkey may sometimes be able to work on a month-by-month basis.

A typical schedule in the Mid East and Turkey involves five days and 20-25 hours of teaching per week, but some employers in the Gulf require teachers to be present at the work site for 35-40 hours per week. Year contracts usually include at least 4 weeks of paid vacation, and there are normally quite a few paid public holidays each year.

Salaries in countries such as Jordan, Syria, Oman, Yemen and Turkey allow a comfortable lifestyle, but they rarely permit savings of more than $200-$300 a month. (Teachers who give extra lessons may be able to save considerably more.) In the Gulf states, salaries often permit savings of $1000-$1500 a month.

Flights and accommodations are almost always arranged and paid for by employers in Kuwait, the UAE and Saudi Arabia but not in the other countries.

Chapter 5

Conducting A TEFL Job Search: 1

- **How To Start Your Job Search**
- **How To Locate Suitable Jobs**

HOW TO START YOUR JOB SEARCH

Why A Logical Approach Is Essential

If you conduct your job search in a haphazard way, you run a large number of risks. You may not get a job at all; or you may miss out on available good jobs and end up getting a mediocre one. You may take a job which you then find you hate, or one which is in a place which you hate. You may have such a miserable time overseas that you break your contract and make an early return home. All of these possibilities are clearly undesirable.

Let me give you some actual examples of problems which I have seen teachers run into because they did not approach their job search with enough care:

- Christine suffered from asthma. She took a job in Jakarta, not realizing that the city has one of the worst air pollution problems in the world. Her asthma was so bad that she had to return to the US after only a month.

- Jordan signed a contract with a school in Taiwan. The contract guaranteed a good hourly rate of pay and mentioned "an average monthly teaching schedule of 110 hours." He had to leave after two months because the school was only able to arrange a monthly teaching load of 20 hours, and he could not live on his salary. (Although his contract guaranteed an hourly rate of pay, it did not in any way guarantee how many hours of teaching would actually be arranged for him.)

- John needed a job which would allow him to send home $500 a month to repay his student loans. He took a suitably highly paid job in Argentina. It was not until he arrived in Buenos Aires that he found out he could not remit his savings on a monthly basis; he could only bring them back to the US as a lump sum at the end of his contract.

- Karen desperately wanted to get a job in Latin America so that she could improve her Spanish. She took a job in Rio de Janeiro. It was a great job in a great place - but she did not get many opportunities to work on her Spanish!

Establishing Your Key Needs

Before even thinking about looking for specific jobs, sit down and make a list of any job or location features which you feel are absolutely essential to you. These are your key needs, and you will need to avoid any job or location which does not meet every single one of them. You may want to use the following questions as a starting point for your list of key needs:

1 Are you prepared to travel overseas to fix up a job, or is it essential that you arrange a job in advance?

2 Do you absolutely need to have your airfare paid?

3 Do you need to save a specific amount during your time abroad?

4 Do you need to be able to remit a certain amount each month to the US or Canada?

5 Do you have any significant health problems, or have any prescription needs, which would rule out certain countries?

6 Could you cope with working in a small town, or are you totally a big city person?

Establishing Preferences

After deciding on your key needs, you should make a second list. This time, list job or location features which, while not essential, would certainly come high on your job "wish list." Again, the following questions may help to get you started:

1 Would you be prepared to work six days a week?

2 Would you be prepared to teach children and adolescents as well as adults?

3 Would you be much happier in a city where you would have easy access to English-language cultural and entertainment events?

4 Would you much prefer not to have to share an apartment?

5 Is it important that you work in a school which provides good educational support and possibilities for teacher development?

Eliminating Unsuitable Locations

The next step in starting your job search is to list all of the countries where you think you would, or even might, like to work and live. Spend some time looking through a world atlas while you do this, and do not worry if you finish up with a very long list.

After that, you need to eliminate all those countries which simply do not meet your all of your key needs. Start by looking at my comments on different areas of the world in Chapter 4: An Overview Of The Job Market. This should give you an idea of which countries have the types of jobs which you are looking for and offer the kind of working conditions which you need. It should quickly eliminate at least a few of the countries on your list.

Next, take some time to find out a little about lifestyle factors in the countries still on your list: climate, geography, culture, etc. The best way to do this is by reading descriptions of the countries in a recent almanac or in an encyclopedia. Look for features which would greatly influence whether you would find life there pleasant or disagreeable. You do not need to do in-depth research at this stage - you are just looking to eliminate obviously unsuitable countries from your list.

Drawing Up A Shortlist Of Possible Locations

By the time you have completed the steps outlined in the section above, you should have gained a general impression of the TEFL job market and have reduced your list of possible job locations to a more reasonable length.

You now need to find out more about the countries which are still on your list, and about the current TEFL job market in those countries. To do this efficiently, you will need to be able to access the Internet. If you do not have a computer with Internet access, you should be able to use one at your local public library.

The following ideas may help you to draw up your shortlist:

* Find out more about the countries from encyclopedias and/or travel guides.

* Look at the country-by-country job information journal on Dave's ESL Cafe (www.eslcafe.com/jobinfo/). Written by people who have taught overseas, the journal entries often provide valuable insights into EFL teachers' lifestyles overseas.

* Check out the comments on the "Job Discussion" page of Dave's ESL Cafe (www.eslcafe.com/jd/). Perhaps make some postings yourself asking for advice from people who have worked in the different countries.

* Check to see whether there is a TEFL job market in each country and, if so, the size of that market. You can do this by looking at the list of employers in Appendix 5. You might also want to do a quick check on current job vacancies by looking at the "Jobs Offered" page of Dave's ESL Cafe (www.eslcafe.com).

* If you are taking a TEFL training course, access the training center's job resources. If you chose the right course, these resources should include cultural briefing notes on different countries, briefing notes produced by overseas schools, sample job contracts, letters from the center's graduates abroad, etc.

Use the information which you gather to produce a prioritized shortlist of target countries, all of which seem to meet your key needs with regards to lifestyles and jobs. You will probably also have found some specific job leads. You are now ready to start looking for jobs and contacting potential employers.

HOW TO FIND AND GET A SUITABLE JOB

Two Very Different Approaches

There are basically two ways to obtain a TEFL job: you can arrange a job in advance from your home country, or you can travel overseas to conduct an in-country job search. I would strongly recommend the former approach, particularly if you have not lived overseas before. In my experience, the better employers generally carry out their recruitment well in advance, rather than hoping that suitable teachers will simply turn up on their doorsteps.

In most cases, teachers who have a recognized TEFL certificate should have no difficulty prearranging jobs from the USA or Canada. However, there are some exceptions. North Americans who want to teach in Western Europe will find that the only way to get a job is by going to the country and conducting a door-to-door job search. Also, some employers in Latin American countries place great importance on meeting prospective job applicants face to face; even though they may negotiate almost all employment details with you over the phone or fax, they may insist on your traveling to the country concerned to sign your contract.

Finding Jobs In-Country

Even if you decide to, or have to, carry out an in-country job search, you should not normally think in terms of just jumping on a plane to your target country. That really is a very risky way to approach a TEFL job search!

In all areas except Western Europe, you will greatly improve your chances of finding a suitable position by first finding out about and then contacting all potential employers in advance. About two months before you travel, send each school director a copy of your resume, together with a cover letter. In the letter, mention your planned arrival date and say that you will contact the employer again on arrival, in the hope that he/she will be interested in meeting you. When you get to the country, mention that you sent in a resume, and ask if you may talk with the director to arrange a time when you can meet him/her.

Arranging Jobs In Advance

To obtain a TEFL job before you leave your home country, you need to be ready to approach potential employers in two very different ways. One way is by responding to advertisements for specific vacancies; these announcements may be placed by employers or by recruitment organizations, acting as agents for employers. The other way is by contacting schools, recruitment agencies and other organizations to ask whether they have, or expect to have in the future, job vacancies of the type which will meet your needs. I will discuss each of these two approaches separately. However, a thorough job search will almost always involve the simultaneous use of both approaches.

Finding And Responding To Job Advertisements

This may be the easiest way to approach your job search, particularly if you are not in a great hurry or if you are looking for work in a really flourishing job market, such as South Korea or Mexico. All you need to do is keep an eye on likely job advertising sources and then respond whenever you see an interesting vacancy, taking care to submit all of the documents which are requested in the advertisement. If you are looking for a job in a very active TEFL market, you will probably find yourself responding to numerous advertisements within a few days.

However, in the case of many job markets, this approach may require a lot of time and patience. For example, although there is a flourishing TEFL market in Argentina, you will see very few advertisements for jobs there. This is because most Argentine schools expect to be approached directly by more potential teachers than they require, and so they do not see a need to advertise vacancies.

Until quite recently, it was extremely difficult to locate TEFL job advertisements: schools simply could not afford the costs involved in advertising in North American or international publications. So if I had been writing this book even two or three years ago, I would have stressed the need for prospective teachers to look for job advertisement in the following sources:

- The 'Jobs Wanted' sections in the Sunday editions of major American or Canadian newspapers.

- The 'Overseas Jobs' sections of British newspapers and periodicals, such as "The Guardian" and "The Times Educational Supplement."

- The 'TEFL Jobs Offered' sections in such foreign newspapers as "The Japan Times."

- The "Job Placement Bulletin" produced by, and available by subscription from, the TESOL association in Alexandria, VA.

All of these publications are still useful sources of job advertisements, but they have been totally overshadowed by the growth of Internet TEFL web sites. The development of the World Wide Web has made it possible for even the smallest overseas schools to make their recruitment needs known quickly and economically to potential teachers all over the world. So with a minimum of effort and expense, anyone with Internet access can find and investigate a huge range of TEFL job vacancies suitable for both trained and untrained teachers.

The Best Sources Of TEFL Job Advertisements

Literally scores of websites claim that they carry details of TEFL job vacancies with a variety of employers around the world, and prospective teachers can waste days on looking through such sites. However, in my experience, only three sites are really worth monitoring on a regular basis. These are:

- The "Jobs Offered" pages of Dave's ESL Cafe (www.eslcafe. com). These pages feature a constantly-changing array of advertisements for TEFL jobs of all types and in all areas of the world. You can quickly scroll through a master list of current vacancies, and then use the hyperlinks supplied to find out more about each vacancy and how to apply for it.

- The job vacancies section of the Digital Education Network's website (www.jobs.edunet.com).
- The job search section of the TEFL Professional Network's website (www.tefl.com/jobs/search/htm).

Another possible source of job advertisements is the International Placement Gazette, which is available from 423 Townes Street, Greenville, SC 29601, USA. The telephone number to contact is: (800) 882-9188. Their website is at: www.intemployment.com.

Teachers who are based in the UK or who are prepared to take out a subscription to a British-based publication will find a wide range of TEFL vacancies advertised in the "ELT Prospects" section of the monthly "EL Gazette." Further details can be obtained from the Gazette's website (www.elgazette.com).

A word of warning about applying for advertised jobs! The advertisements on websites or in publications are not screened in any way and so the jobs offered (and the employers who offer them) reflect the full spectrum of the TEFL market, with perhaps an emphasis on jobs open to untrained teachers. Inevitably, this means that some of the positions offer extremely poor salaries and working conditions, and many may involve working for unethical and exploitative employers. So it is very important that you approach the vacancies with caution - as you should approach all TEFL job vacancies, in fact. Before signing a contract for any of these jobs, you should read the section on "Evaluating Job Offers" in Chapter 7 of this book.

Credentialed teachers can find advertisements for appropriate overseas positions in The International Educator. This can be obtained by contacting TIE at P O Box 513, Cummaquid, MA 02637, USA (website: www.tieonline.com).

Contacting Potential Employers "Cold"

Another and very different way to approach your job search is by contacting potential employers who are not currently advertising specific jobs. This approach is probably the best approach to use if you want a job in a specific town, or in a country for which you rarely see job advertisements.

Contacting potential employers "cold" is a very simple process. All you need to do is to find names and addresses of employers in your target area, and then to send them a copy of your resume together with a suitable cover letter. If they have a job vacancy, or expect to have one in the near future, they will contact you with details. If they do not, they will probably tell you when they expect to have jobs and when you should contact them again.

You can find a list of addresses of possible employers around the world in Appendix 5. You will find detailed advice on how to write a suitable resume and cover letter in Chapter 6.

The Most Economical Approach

If you are at all flexible with regard to possible job locations, the most economical approach is to contact some of the larger TEFL school groups and recruitment organizations or agencies, rather than to approach individual schools. This is because a single application to a major school group or recruitment organization will usually put you in line for any one of a hundred or more jobs.

As most large school groups and recruitment agencies have their own application forms and processes, it normally is not appropriate to send a resume. It is usually better to contact the organization to ask for details of vacancies and a copy of their application documents.

You will find a list of large school groups and recruitment organizations in Appendix 4.

Some Points To Bear In Mind

If you decide to carry out a "cold" job search by contacting individual schools, here are some important points to remember:

1 To be successful, you will probably need to send out a fairly large number of resumes and cover letters, since many of the employers whom you contact will not have any suitable vacancies. Ideally, you will write to every one of the potential employers in your target area or areas. In the case of a large city or a small country, you may well have to contact 20 or more organiza-

tions; in the case of a larger country with a strong EFL market, you may have to contact 50 or more organizations.

2 As explained in Chapter 6, all that you should initially send to each potential employer is a brief cover letter and resume. (This is perhaps just as well, given the large number of organizations you may need to contact.)

3 You need to be patient, as it may take several weeks for your letters to reach their destinations, for them to be considered, and for responses to reach you. If your letters happen to arrive during a busy period or while there is an extended public holiday overseas, this may slow the process down even more. So do not worry if you do not receive replies within two or three weeks. Also, do not start sending follow-up letters for at least one month after your original mailing, as this will tend to irritate many employers!

4 If you have not received a reply within about four or five weeks, it is perfectly acceptable to send a follow-up letter to each potential employer. However, you have to be very careful how you phrase any such letter, so as to avoid appearing too presumptuous or aggressive.

Chapter 6

Conducting A TEFL Job Search: 2

- **Producing An Effective TEFL Resume**
- **Writing A Cover Letter That Works**

AN EFFECTIVE TEFL RESUME

Introduction

Depending upon how you approach potential employers, you may need to produce two different versions of your resume. If you are approaching employers "cold," you should draw up a resume of the type described below. However, if you are responding to a job advertisement, you need to follow closely any and all instructions which the advertisement gives with regard to the production and submission of your resume.

Producing An Effective TEFL Resume

It is important to realize that overseas TEFL employers will usually not be comfortable with, or impressed by, the types of resume which are normal for jobs in North America.

On the one hand, your TEFL resume needs to be very short: not more than one side of paper. This is because overseas TEFL employers are extremely busy and they will be turned off by long resumes; if they

73

want more information on some aspect of your qualifications, they will ask you for it at some stage.

On the other hand, it absolutely has to include a number of personal details which usually would not be included in a resume for use with employers in the USA or Canada. You may be reluctant to include these details. However, if you do not put them in your resume, you are really very unlikely to receive a favorable response.

You should read the following comments about the format and content of a TEFL resume for use with overseas employers. You should then draw up your own resume using as a guide the example which I give.

Basic Features Of A TEFL Resume

TEFL resumes are usually written in English. However, if you have a good command of the language used in the school area, you might want to produce a "foreign language" version. In this case, be sure to have this version checked and corrected by a native speaker. Then use it to produce a bilingual resume: English on one side and the other language on the other side.

Your resume, which should not cover more than one side of paper, ought to be typed on white paper. It should be laid out clearly and neatly. If you use a word processor, avoid using too many different font types and sizes. Also, leave reasonably wide left and right hand margins: a 1" margin is ideal.

When you have produced a suitable original (which, as I will explain below should include a recent photograph), take it to a good photocopy store and have plenty of copies made on normal 20-pound paper. I would advise against having your resume copied onto any kind of special paper: some employers will be worried if they think you are so insecure about your writing skills that you have had your resume professionally produced.

Essential Elements

Your resume needs to include all of the following elements, for the reasons which I give below:

- A small passport-type photo:
  This is standard practice in most countries; if you do not attach a photo, employers will assume that you have something to hide. Any small picture (even black and white) will do, as long as it is clear; for example, the pictures produced by photo booths are perfectly acceptable. However, make sure that you look as respectable as possible in the photo! Men should avoid wearing any jewelry and should tie long hair back out of sight. Both men and women should avoid being photographed wearing any type of "exotic" face jewelry, such as nose studs or tongue rings.

- Your current citizenship:
  This is to enable employers to see at a glance whether you are legally eligible to receive a work permit in their country.

- Mention of the fact that English is your mother tongue:
  This is particularly important if you have a non-English-sounding name, because most employers are very reluctant to recruit EFL teachers who are not native English speakers.

- Your country and date of birth:
  This is standard practice overseas, because these details may well affect whether or not you will eligible to receive a work permit.

- Your marital status:
  For present purposes this is simply either "single" or "married." If you are going to be accompanied by children, mention them and their ages, also. It is very important for employers to know whether they will have to help you to obtain residence visas for dependents, and what type of housing you are going to need.

- Brief details of your formal educational qualifications:
  If you have a degree, give only the date, type of degree, major and institution. Do not include details of your GPA, etc. If you have other diplomas or certificates, give similarly brief details. Unless you do not have a degree, you need not include details of your high school education.

- Brief details of any TEFL/TESL training you have had.

- Brief details of any previous TEFL/TESL experience:
  This should include mention of any tutoring which you may have done. Express this as shown in the sample resume given below.

- A brief summary of any other previous work experience:
  In the case of jobs with no relevance to TEFL, include only ones which lasted for a significant period of time. Highlight any of your work experience which may be particularly relevant to TEFL: for example, jobs involving teaching, training, dealing with the public, or interacting with non-English speakers. Do not explain the jobs or the duties, skills, etc. involved, except in cases where the job was of an unusual type.

- Brief mentions of any skills or other experience which you feel are relevant to teaching EFL overseas:
  These may include such things as: languages studied or learned; international travel; periods of residence overseas; computer skills. Details of overseas travel and residencies are particularly important, as they will reassure employers that you are not likely to become so homesick that you will break your contract and return home after a few weeks of living and working overseas.

You should not enclose copies of reference letters or testimonials with your resume. Instead, include a line saying that you will send references upon request. (Incidentally, employers in most countries do not attach much significance to open letters of reference from previous employers, etc. In these days of computers and laser printers, it is too easy to produce such letters yourself!)

A Note On References

Although you do not need to include references in your resume, this is a good time to think about and approach people who might provide references when you need them. The best references are from past or current TEFL employers or, failing this, from other past or current employers. If you do not have any real work experience, you should ask some of your college professors. Contact possible referees now to ask if you may use them. Also, make sure that you have an accurate list of their current addresses and phone/fax numbers.

A Sample Resume

Fred William Smith
P. O. Box 123
Palo Alto, CA 94306, USA
Tel: (415) 493-0000
E-mail: smith999@aol.com

Personal Details

Birth: USA, 10/29/1974
Marital Status: Single
Citizenship: US
Mother Tongue: English

Education

2000   BA (English)
         California State University, Hayward, California, USA

TEFL/TESL Training

2002   Cambridge Certificate in TEFL, Pass Grade
         English International, San Francisco

TEFL/TESL Experience

2002   Part-time ESL tutor, Tutoring Inc., Los Angeles. May-July.
         4 hours a week with intermediate students.

Other Work Experience

2000-03 Library Assistant, Stanford University, Palo Alto, USA
1996-99 Temporary jobs to finance education: waiter, taxi driver, etc.

Relevant Skills & Experience

Foreign Languages: Italian (Elementary)
Overseas Travel: Italy, Spain, Mexico, Brazil, India, Japan
Overseas Residencies: Ireland (3 months in 1995)
Associations: TESOL

References

Available upon request

77

WRITING A COVER LETTER

The Importance Of The Cover Letter

Whether you send or take your resume to potential employers, you will need to attach a cover letter, addressed to the director of the target organization. As employers will usually look at this even before reading your resume, you need to ensure that this letter will create a good first impression.

The first point that you have to bear in mind is that school directors tend to be very busy people who receive a large number of unsolicited job inquiry letters and resumes. So your inquiry will stand a much better chance of being read and considered seriously if it is brief and clear. Directors simply will not be prepared to spend time reading a long cover letter or resume, or looking through a stack of transcripts, etc. They expect to be able to glance at a cover letter and to see at once whether the writer meets the school's basic employment requirements.

The second point to remember is that you are applying for a job as a teacher of English. So it is really crucial that your letter be accurate and appropriate in terms of grammatical usage, vocabulary choice, spelling, and punctuation. If you make any mistakes in your letter, you will immediately eliminate yourself from consideration.

A Checklist Of Key Points

I would suggest that you base your inquiry letter on the sample given on the next page, and that you take into account all of the points mentioned below:

- Keep your letter to no more than one side of paper.

- Write your letter clearly in simple English. This is because a great many TEFL employers themselves speak only a limited amount of English and therefore a more complex letter may just confuse them.

- If you speak the language of the country concerned, you might want to produce a bilingual letter: English on one side, the foreign other language on the other.

- Make absolutely sure that your letter does not contain any mistakes of grammar, spelling or punctuation. Remember that you are applying for a job as a teacher of English! (The very worst mistake that you can make is to write "English" without a capital letter: most employers feel quite strongly that people who cannot spell "English" should not be allowed to teach it!)

- The cover letter should normally be typed or word-processed.

- Produce an original on white paper and then make multiple copies on standard 20-pound paper.

- Sign each copy individually, preferably using blue or black ink.

- If you are word-processing a lot of letters to send to schools in different countries or towns, proofread them carefully. (I have seen letters addressed to schools in Paris which mention how much the writer would enjoy living in Spain!)

- Avoid using too assertive a tone: what Americans see as being "assertive" all too often comes across to people from other countries as being "aggressive." Overseas employers expect job applicants to be (or at least to appear to be) fairly humble! Expressions such as "I look forward to an early reply" or "I am looking forward to working for your school" will offend more employers than they will impress.

- When mentioning the type of work which you are seeking, try to sound flexible and open-minded. (See the fifth paragraph of the sample letter below.) Most EFL employers want teachers who are willing to teach a range of different ages and language levels.

- Include some mention of why you would like to work in the particular country or town, but try not to sound too insincerely enthusiastic. (See paragraph four in the following letter.)

A Sample Cover Letter

1200 Baker Street
San Francisco
CA 94114, USA

The Director
Escuela Lincoln
11 Avenida Bolivar,
Quito 1542, Ecuador   January 12, 2003

Dear Director:

I am hoping to find work as a teacher of English in Quito from
October. I would be grateful if you would send me details of any
vacancies which you expect to have in your school at that time.

As you will see from my resume, I am an American citizen and a
university graduate. I am a native speaker of English, and I hold the
Cambridge Certificate in English Language Teaching to Adults
(CELTA), with a 'Pass' Grade.

Although I do not have any formal EFL teaching experience, I have
carried out fifty hours of ESL tutoring of adult immigrants from
Mexico and Guatemala.

I visited Ecuador in 2001 and I was impressed by the beauty of the
country and character of its people. I would like to return, this time
to work, in order to learn more about the country and its culture.

I would prefer a full-time position for 12 months, but I would
certainly consider part-time or temporary work. I would be happy to
teach both adults and children, although I have no experience of
working with younger learners.

I will be grateful for any information which you can send me.

Sincerely,

Andrea Braun

Chapter 7

Conducting A TEFL Job Search: 3

- **Getting Suitable Job Offers**
- **How To Evaluate Job Offers**
- **Accepting & Rejecting Job Offers**

GETTING SUITABLE JOB OFFERS

Job Interviews

The situation with regard to the interviewing of applicants for TEFL jobs overseas varies a great deal depending upon the preferences of the individual employers concerned. If you hold a TEFL certificate which is internationally recognized, you may well not have to go through any kind of job interview at all: many employers will rely solely on the fact that you are certified or on a reference from the center where you were trained. At the other end of the spectrum, some of the large TEFL recruitment organizations require all applicants, trained or untrained, to participate in a series of interviews, some of which may last for several hours.

The most common arrangement lies somewhere between these two extremes: you will be required to participate in a 30-60 minute interview with a representative of the school or recruitment agency to which you have applied. The interview may be carried out face-to-face or over the telephone; in some cases, it may even be carried out by fax or e-mail.

The Importance of First Impressions

Research shows that interviewers form a judgement about applicants within the first 3-5 minutes of an interview. This initial impression rarely changes, no matter what happens in the rest of the interview. So the key to successful interviewing is to make the best possible impression in those crucial first few minutes. The following points should help you to do this.

Any organized and professional interviewer will already have looked over your application documents and will have started forming an impression of your suitability even before your interview begins. So, when applying for jobs, make sure that your resume and other application documents are well presented.

The very worst thing you can do is to arrive late for a face-to-face interview, or not to be available at the arranged time in the case of a phone interview. Whatever your reason or excuse, if you are even a few minutes late, you are extremely unlikely to be successful. So make sure you are in the right place at least 10-15 minutes early. Apart from ensuring that you are punctual, this will give you time to calm your nerves and to prepare yourself psychologically for the start of the interview: you certainly do not want to start an interview when you are still short of breath from a last minute rush through traffic!

Physical appearance counts a lot, even in the most informal of interviews. Remember that the interviewer is evaluating you for a job which involves standing up in front of fee-paying students. Remember, too, that he/she will assume that you have made a special effort with your appearance for the interview and that you would dress a little less well for work! So wear appropriately formal clothes: a jacket and tie for men, and a dress or skirt and blouse for women. Avoid all forms of exotic body-piercing jewelry, such as nose rings; if you are a man, do not wear earrings. Men with long hair should make sure that it looks as tidy as possible: this usually means tying it back. Women should avoid bright nail polish, and both men and women should make sure that their hands and nails are clean.

You should remember to make a special effort to speak clearly and to avoid using too many slang expressions. Always remember that you are applying for a job to teach English!

More Advice On Interviews

Although it is impossible to predict the exact course which interviews will take, you can and should spend some time preparing yourself for some of the questions which you might be asked, and for some which you may be expected to ask. In particular, you need to demonstrate that you have given serious thought to the job, the school, and the country concerned.

I would strongly recommend that you take the following nine steps before attending any TEFL job interview:

- Do some research on the country and city where you hope to work. You do not have to be an expert, but you should know some basic facts about: population, culture, language, religion, etc. Any good travel guide or encyclopedia will help with this.

- Read carefully any information which the school sent you about the job, the school's students, etc.

- Be sure to brush up your knowledge of English grammar. Whether you are trained or untrained, you are almost certain to be asked to demonstrate a reasonable understanding of basic English grammar: for example, the use of a particular verb tense or the difference between two similar structures. (Most employers and students overseas place a very high priority on grammatical knowledge, and they expect EFL teachers to be familiar with basic grammar terms and structures.)

- If you do not have TEFL/TESL training, look through some relevant EFL course books to get an idea of the types of activities which are used in EFL classrooms. If the information sent to you by the school mentions specific EFL course books, try to get copies to look at. Otherwise, look through one of the main TEFL coursebooks, such as "New Interchange" by Jack Richards.

- You are very likely to be asked for your ideas on how to teach various vocabulary or grammatical items, or on how to practice reading, listening or speaking skills. If you have done a TEFL training course, this should not cause you any problems. If you are untrained, you should read an introductory book on TEFL methodology. Details of suitable books are given in Chapter 2.

- Be ready to say why you think you would be an effective teacher: you have good interpersonal skills, you are good at explaining things, etc. When doing this, be careful not to exaggerate your skills or accomplishments, in case you are asked to demonstrate them. For example, if you say that you speak a particular language "fluently," the interviewer might just decide to carry out the rest of the interview in that language!

- Be equally ready to say (if asked) which aspects of the job and life overseas might take you time to come to grips with: holding down the amount you talk in class, learning the local language, etc. Naturally, express confidence that you would be able to handle these problems, but show that you are sensible enough to realize life will not be all smooth sailing.

- Prepare a list of questions which you would like to ask. Here it is important not to start with questions about the salary and the contract. You want to come across as being interested in doing the best possible job, rather than in getting the best possible conditions of work. So start by asking about the school, its students and its teachers. Ask about what kind of classes and students you would teach. Then ask what aspects of work and life other foreign teachers have enjoyed most or found most difficult. Only after covering these areas should you ask about salary, vacations, etc. (See the section on "Evaluating Job Offers" later in this chapter.)

- Be careful about how you phrase all your questions, and particularly any which relate to salary and working conditions. It is very important that you come across as being naturally interested and curious, rather than skeptical or suspicious.

What To Bring With You To An Interview

Although you will probably already have submitted a resume, you should bring an extra copy with you to the interview because many interviewers have been known to lose applicants' resumes! If possible, you should also bring with you the originals and photocopies of all relevant documents: degree diploma, TEFL certificate, and letters of reference (or names and addresses of referees).

HOW TO EVALUATE JOB OFFERS

The Need To Clarify Job Offers

I have known many EFL teachers who were so excited at receiving a job offer that they accepted the job without reading the offer carefully. In most cases, these teachers regretted their haste when they later had problems with their employers over points which were not clearly stated in the job offer or contract. So whenever you receive a job offer, remember that you need to read and think about it carefully before you accept it and sign a formal contract.

In my experience, you will almost certainly have to ask employers for some clarification of a job offer/contract before you can really decide whether the job meets your needs. The comments and questions listed below cover a whole range of areas which you need to clarify about any TEFL job which you are considering. Every single item on the list relates to an issue which I have known to cause problems for teachers in the past.

Of course, you will not have to ask direct questions about all the issues on the list! Most of the points will be clearly addressed in the written job offer/contract provided by the employer, or they will have been explained during pre-interview communications with the employer. Still more will no doubt be raised and clarified by the interviewer. So just use my checklist to make sure that, by the time you finally sign a contract, you fully understand what you are committing yourself to and what working conditions you can expect.

Be Careful!

Even after receiving a definite job offer, you will usually need to clarify some aspects of the job. At this point, it is essential not to offend the employer by appearing too suspicious. I would recommend the following approach. After receiving the offer, contact the employer by fax or e-mail (so you have a written record of responses). Say that you are very happy with and excited by the offer, but that there are some minor points which you do not quite understand and which you would like to ask about, to avoid possible misunderstandings.

A Useful Checklist

Contract Length

A one year contract is standard for most jobs, but you need to check the exact dates involved.

- How long is your contract?
- Does it start on your arrival in the overseas country, or on your first day of work?

Salary

Salaries are usually paid at the end of each calendar month and in local currency. They are normally paid net of local taxes.

- What is the minimum gross monthly salary which you are guaranteed to receive irrespective of your actual hours of work?
- What is the net salary (after taxes, etc.)?
- When is the salary paid?
- Are there any bonus payments at the end of contract? If so, how much will you receive net, and when will you receive it?
- How much of your salary, if any, will you be legally able to send out of the country?

Other Benefits

These vary enormously from job to job and country to country. You can get an idea of the prevailing benefits situation in different countries and regions by reading Chapter 4: An Overview Of The Job Market.

- Will you be covered by public or private health insurance? If so, when does the coverage start, and who pays for it? If not, how can you arrange health insurance and how much is it likely to cost?
- What public or school holidays are there? Are you paid for them?
- How much paid annual vacation do you get? Can you choose when to take this, or is it decided by the school?
- Will the school pay your airfare out to the country? Will it pay your fare home at the end of your contract?

- Will the school pay for you to bring any excess baggage?
- Will the school provide housing? If not, will it help you to find suitable accommodations?
- Is housing paid by the employer? If so, are utilities included?
- If housing is not paid by the school, how much rent will you probably have to pay each month?
- Will housing usually be furnished?
- Will you have to pay any kind of security or rent deposit? If so, how much will you pay, and when will it be returned to you?
- Will you be able to live alone, or will you have to share housing?
- If you have to share housing, will you have a room of your own?
- Will the school provide lessons in the local language?

Working Hours

Most of the better schools offer a weekly teaching schedule of 20-30 hours; however, some require up to 35-40 hours, particularly if you will be working from a detailed lesson manual rather than having to plan your own lessons.

A 5-day week is fairly standard in Europe and Latin America, but a 6-day week is common elsewhere. A split schedule (some mornings and some afternoons or evenings) is fairly typical, but you should avoid jobs which require you to teach lessons at several widely differing times throughout the day. Similarly, you should beware of jobs which require you to teach at many different locations each day.

Some schools offer a lot of overtime work paid at special rates. You may well want to do such work, especially after you have settled in to your normal teaching schedule. However, it is very risky to accept a contract with compulsory overtime. One teacher whom I know went to Turkey on a contract which specified a 20-hour weekly teaching schedule, but which included a compulsory overtime clause. She ended up teaching 35 hours a week for the full six months of her contract. She saved a lot of money, but she did not enjoy her teaching - and she never got to see any of the country!

- How many school "hours" per week will you be required to teach? How many minutes are in a school hour?
- What is your likely weekly schedule?

- Will you be required to carry out any additional work apart from normal lesson planning and homework marking? If so, what is this work, and how much of it will there be?
- Apart from your teaching hours, are there any other times when you will be required to be present on the school premises?
- Where will you be teaching?
- If you will be teaching outside of the school, who will pay your travel costs? Will you also be paid travel time?
- Is overtime likely to be available? If so, how many hours, and at what rate of pay?
- Is overtime work compulsory?

Educational Conditions

Life is easier, and you will develop much more as a teacher, in a school which has a good educational infrastructure and which offers educational support to its teachers.

It is also better to work for schools which are well organized. For example, you will find the teaching is easier in a school which divides students into at least four or five different levels; this is because you will not have to teach classes which contain a wide range of abilities. Well-organized schools also tend to give each new teacher several classes of the same level, in order to reduce the teacher's lesson planning load.

- How many levels are students divided into?
- How many different class levels will you probably teach?
- Are classes based on assigned coursebooks, or will you be expected to provide all your own lesson plans and materials?
- What is the age range of students in each class?
- Will you have to teach separate classes of adults, adolescents, or children?
- Will you have access to a Course Coordinator or someone similar who can advise you on lesson planning, how to deal with class problems, etc.?
- Will you receive any orientation or briefing when you arrive and before you teach your first classes?
- Will you be able to observe classes before you start teaching?

• Does the school schedule regular faculty meetings at which educational issues are discussed?

ACCEPTING & REJECTING JOB OFFERS

The Need To Be Professional And Ethical

If you carry out your job search in the way shown in this book, you should receive multiple job offers. It is very important that you handle these offers in a professional way, and that you try to avoid misleading and inconveniencing employers by "collecting" unsuitable job offers.

Of course, this is not to say that you should not hold onto a job offer for a reasonable time. For example, it is quite acceptable to hold onto a possibly suitable offer if you have a reasonable hope of receiving a better one from another employer in the near future. However, if you receive an offer which is clearly totally unsuitable, the only ethical action is to contact the employer as soon as possible to say that you appreciate the offer but that you will not be accepting the job. By doing this, you free the employer to start considering other applicants, some of whom may really want and need the job.

You may sometimes be in the position of being pressured by one employer to accept an offer quickly while you would prefer to wait for a while for another offer. Or you may receive two possibly suitable offers at once and may want to have some time to consider both offers. In such cases, it is best to be straight with the employers. They should not be offended if you contact them to say that, while you appreciate their offer, you have some reservations and so need a little time to consider it. No reasonable employer (and you would not want to work for an unreasonable one) will be offended even if you say you need time to consider their offer because you have received an attractive offer from another school.

The Need to be Polite

At some point, you are likely to receive a job offer which is either totally unsuitable or which is simply not as good as another offer which you have already received. In both cases, you will presumably contact the relevant employer to reject their offer. At this point, you would be well advised to reject the offer in as polite a way as possible. Why? Because you cannot be sure that you will not want to be considered again by the employer, perhaps for a different job at a much later date; and employers tend to have long memories. Let me give you an example of what can happen.

Marilyn received job offers from School A and School B. She accepted School B's offer, which was markedly better. She then wrote a strong letter to School A, basically saying that their offer was pitiful and that she would never consider working for such an inferior organization. Three months later, School A took over School B. The teacher did not lose her job, but she soon found out that her future promotion prospects were - zero.

So, even when rejecting job offers, it pays to be polite and professional in your dealings with employers.

Chapter 8

Legalities, Practicalities & Health

- **Legal Requirements & Considerations**
- **Books, Clothes & Other Items To Bring**
- **Health & Medical Preparations**

LEGAL REQUIREMENTS & CONSIDERATIONS

Residence Visas & Work Permits

If you are going to live and work in any foreign country, you need to obtain two basic documents: a residence visa and a work permit. The residence visa allows you to stay in the country for more than the three month period usually permitted by a tourist visa. The work permit allows you to work legally in the country. Normally, you have to get an employment contract before you can get a work permit; and you must have a work permit before you can get a residence visa. If you stay in a country without a valid visa, you are breaking the law. If you work in a country without having a work permit, you are also breaking the law.

The regulations for visas and work permits vary greatly from country to country (and sometimes even month to month), as do the penalties for breaking local visa and permit laws. The comments below cover some of the main considerations and possibilities.

Prearranged Jobs

If you prearrange an overseas job from North America, the employer will usually handle the legalities for you, provided that you supply him/her with the necessary documents. You will then receive the visa and/or work permit either in your home country or on arrival in the foreign country.

In some cases, particularly if the employer needs a teacher urgently, he/she may ask you to enter the overseas country on a tourist visa. The employer will then arrange for you to receive a work permit and to exchange your tourist visa for a residence visa after you have entered the country. He/She will inform you of the documents which you will need to bring with you.

Employers will tell you which documents you will need to provide in order for them to obtain your visa and permit. These normally include the following:

- a current passport with at least one year of validity;
- a legal copy of your birth certificate;
- a legal copy of your college/university diploma;
- a number (often 6-10) small passport-style photos.

There may be additional requirements depending upon the country where you will be working.

- Some countries require that you provide a medical certificate or statement confirming that you are in good health; other countries may insist that you undergo a full medical examination on arrival. In both cases, you may well have to undergo a chest X-ray and an HIV test.
- For some countries, you may also have to produce a "clearance" certificate from your local police stating that you have never been convicted of a felony.
- If you are going to a Muslim country, you may have to provide a baptism certificate or other evidence that you are not an atheist.
- For some countries, you may have to provide evidence that you have obtained specific TEFL/TESL training.

If this list of possible legal requirements seems overwhelming, you should bear in mind that very few countries require all of the above documents. You should remember also that your employer will advise you on which documents are needed for the specific country.

Arranging Jobs Locally

If you intend to find a job after traveling to a foreign country, you will have to enter that country on a tourist visa. If you intend to work legally, you will need to obtain the relevant work permit and residence visa once you have signed an employment contract.

Theoretically, you should not start work until after you have actually received the necessary permit. However, the authorities in many countries will turn a blind eye provided that you have applied for your permit by the time you start your job. Once your work permit has been issued, you may have to travel to a neighboring country (or occasionally back to your home country) in order to collect your residence visa.

To obtain the necessary permit and visa, you will normally have to provide many of the documents mentioned on the previous page. Some of these can be obtained overseas, but it will make life easier if you bring with you:

- a current passport with at least one year of validity;
- a legal copy of your birth certificate;
- a legal copy of your college/university diploma;
- a legal copy of your TEFL/TESL certificate (if you have such a certificate);
- about 10 small passport-style photos.

Working Illegally

Many teachers work overseas, sometimes for years, without obtaining either a work permit or a residence visa. This practice is particularly common in areas where local attitudes to the law are very relaxed (e.g., in many Latin American or Asian countries), or countries where it is virtually impossible for North Americans to work legally (such as the EU countries of Western Europe).

If you choose to work illegally, you should realize that you will have no legal rights as an employee or a resident and that, if caught, you may face stiff fines and/or other penalties, including deportation.

In general terms, it is very risky to undertake illegal work anywhere

93

for more than a few months, or to work illegally at all in any country in North Africa or the Mid East.

Other Legal Considerations

When you live overseas, you should bear in mind that you are fully subject to local laws, even though you may not approve of those laws. If you break local laws, you will face whatever punishment is normal in the country concerned. Your embassy will usually provide you with legal assistance but it cannot protect you from the consequences of any illegal actions which you have taken.

Most expatriates never face any legal problems whatsoever in foreign countries. However, some North American teachers have gotten themselves into serious trouble; some have even gone to prison for long periods of time.

My advice is to be as scrupulous as possible about respecting local laws, particularly in your first few months when you are unfamiliar with local attitudes. I would be particularly careful with regard to the following areas:

- importing or using drugs in any country (even in countries where drugs are commonly, and even publicly, used by local citizens);
- being openly critical of the government or the military in any authoritarian country;
- drinking alcohol in any country which has prohibition laws;
- breaking any sexual conduct laws (particularly in North Africa and the Mid East).

BOOKS, CLOTHES & OTHER ITEMS TO BRING

I hope this section will help you to decide which items you really need to bring with you to the country where you will be working. When making your decisions, you need to realize that you probably will not be able to bring with you everything that you would like to bring. Apart from other considerations, you will have to bear in mind the baggage limitations imposed by airlines. North American airline companies usually allow you to travel from or to the USA and Canada with a large amount of baggage. However, other airlines are often less generous. Also, when traveling between countries overseas, you will find that all airlines limit you to 44 pounds of baggage; if you go over this limit, you will have to pay very high excess baggage charges.

Books & Teaching Materials

If you are going to teach in a reputable school in a developed country, you should be able to assume that the school will have a reasonable stock of EFL books and other necessary materials. However, you may not be allowed to take these materials out of the school or to access them outside of normal school hours. So you may still want to bring along your own copies of some key EFL books as this will allow you to plan lessons when and where you want. These will probably include an ESL dictionary and a grammar reference.

If you are going to teach in a less developed country or intend to do a lot of private teaching, you will need to bring along a wider selection of EFL reference books, coursebooks and supplementary books.

You can find a list of recommended EFL books, and where to buy them, in Chapter 2.

Clothes & Personal Items

If you have never previously visited the country where you will be working, it will be difficult for you to know which clothes and other personal items to bring with you. The ideal solution is to talk with another American or Canadian who lives in the country or who lived there recently, as he/she will be able to tell you which things are available (at what price) there. If you are going to a prearranged job, ask your employer if they can put you in contact with a current or former teacher from Canada or the USA. If this is not possible or if you are not going to a prearranged job, try to get advice through one of the ESL discussion websites, such as the Jobs Discussion page of Dave's ESL Cafe (www.eslcafe.com/jd/).

Apart from clothes, you may want to bring with you some of the following types of personal items:

- Postcards, maps, etc. of your home town/state. (Students will be very interested in where you come from.)
- Family photos. (As well as being of value to you, these will fascinate your students.)
- Personal items to make you comfortable. (See page 104 for some ideas.)
- Things which are important to you but which you cannot get easily in your target country; for example, specific cosmetics or vitamins.

You may also want to bring some items which you could give as small presents to people such as your landlord's children and the school receptionist. People overseas generally appreciate any items which are clearly from your home country, particularly if they have English writing on them. Pens, keyrings, baseball caps, T-shirts and lipsticks are always welcomed.

Whenever I travel abroad to work, I bring a duty-free bottle of whisky and carton of American cigarettes. I find that these make excellent gifts for people who are particularly kind or helpful to me.

Computers & Devices

Computers are much less common and much more expensive in most overseas countries than they are in North America and you may well not have access to one in the school where you work. If you are going to find it difficult to live without easy computer access, you might want to consider bringing a computer with you.

I would suggest that you check out the computer and e-mail access situation with your employer. You will probably find that the school has some computers but that you will have access to them only at limited times during school hours. In this case, you may want to bring along a laptop and a portable printer. (The latter will not be necessary if the school will allow you to print off your documents on the school's printers. However, you should check that your hardware and software are compatible with the school's printers.)

The following comments may help you to decide which other devices to bring with you:

- If you want to bring a camcorder or video cassettes, check that these will be compatible with the video system used in the overseas country. The American NTSC format is not widely used abroad.

- Audio cassettes and CD's work everywhere.

- Cassette/CD players are comparatively expensive in most countries and so you may want to bring along a portable one. This will be particularly useful if you intend to do private teaching.

- Cameras and film are much more expensive in most countries than they are in Canada and the USA.

- Power systems vary a lot from country to country. Before bringing any electrical device overseas, find out whether it will work in the foreign country and whether it will need an adapter.

Some Other Considerations

As mentioned earlier in this chapter, your airline may operate a very limited baggage allowance. If you are going to exceed this, you should ask whether you can send some of your baggage as "unaccompanied baggage." Under this arrangement, which costs comparatively little, your extra items will not travel with you but will be sent a few days earlier or later. You then have to collect them from the airport a few days after your arrival.

If you intend to bring a computer, check with your employer whether you are likely to be charged customs duties. Most countries now seem to allow laptops to enter free of charge but this is still not the case everywhere.

It generally is not a good idea to leave stuff behind to be mailed on to you when you are overseas. Postal rates are expensive and it is not uncommon in many parts of the world for parcels to disappear on arrival in the overseas country. If you intend to have parcels mailed to you, ask your employer (tactfully) about the reliability of the mail service.

HEALTH & MEDICAL PREPARATIONS

Unless you are traveling to really remote areas, you should not have to worry too much about exotic health risks. However, you could well have some health problems abroad, particularly if you are going to be living or traveling in less-developed countries, and you should take some basic precautions.

The advice which is given below is not a substitute for professional advice from qualified medical personnel, and you should certainly seek such advice before traveling overseas.

Medical Insurance

Most countries have some type of public healthcare system and you should be eligible to use this, provided that you are working legally. Some overseas employers also arrange private health insurance for their expatriate teachers, either to supplement the public system or to cover teachers from the time they arrive until the time they are fully eligible for public healthcare. You should check with your employer in advance to make sure that you will be fully covered from the day you arrive in the overseas country.

If you are not traveling to a prearranged job, you should certainly consider taking out medical insurance from your home country. Any competent insurance broker should be able to arrange this for you, or you can arrange your own coverage through a company such as: Wallach & Company, Inc., 107 W. Federal St., P O Box 480, Middleburg, VA 20118-0480, USA.

Other Preparations

If you have any significant pre-existing medical condition, you should find out whether this is likely to be a serious problem overseas. For example, you should research whether the condition is likely to be aggravated by local climate, altitude and air quality conditions.

If you require any prescribed drugs, you should check that these are readily available in the foreign country. You should also take with you a reasonable supply of any such prescribed drugs. As Canadian and US prescriptions will not be honored abroad, it would be wise to ask your doctor for a letter describing in generic trade and dosage terms what drugs you need and why you need them.

Whether you have any preexisting health problems or not, I would strongly recommend that you undergo a thorough medical check up before you travel. If possible, you should do this at least two months before your planned departure date. It is much better to find out about problems, and probably to have them treated, before you travel than when you are overseas.

Different people feel very differently about the need for vaccinations and immunizations. I personally never worry about obtaining all of the possible shots but I always make sure that I am protected against tuberculosis, polio and tetanus. If I were traveling to a less-developed country, I would also have gamma globulin shots as a protection against hepatitis. As far as other diseases are concerned, I would recommend that you consult your doctor or the Center for Disease Control website (www.cdc.gov) to find out if any additional shots are currently recommended for the country to which you are traveling.

You can find a list of travel clinics, and a lot of other useful health information at the following website: www.tripprep.com/Index.html.

When You Are Overseas

Unless you are unlucky or are traveling to a very remote location, your body's normal defenses and a little common sense should protect you from most major health problems. However, at some time or other you are almost certain to suffer from minor problems such as stomach upset and diarrhea. Some such problems are virtually inevitable given that you will be living in a new environment and will be exposed to different climate, foods, etc.

Some expatriates try to protect themselves against all possible health problems by taking extreme measures, such as refusing to eat food that has not been soaked in iodine. In my experience, such extreme measures are rarely necessary or totally effective. In addition, they will inevitably isolate you from local people, local restaurants, etc.

Your doctor or a traveler's health clinic should be able to advise you on basic precautions to take overseas. Their advice will probably include some or all of the following points:

- You can avoid many health problems by maintaining a high standard of personal hygiene. In particular, you should take care to wash your hands very frequently.

- Avoid too much exposure to the sun, particularly during your first weeks abroad and if you are not used to living in a hot climate. If you have to be in the hot sun, cover your head and wear sunglasses.

- If you are in an area where tap water is of doubtful quality, drink bottled water for the first few days and ask for drinks without ice.

- In most countries, avoid eating dishes made with mayonnaise as this is the most common transmitter of food poisoning.

- Do not eat prepared foods from street or market stands where the food has been kept in the open for a long period of time.

- Avoid eating or drinking any dairy products which have not been pasteurized.

- Wear shoes or sandals at all times when you are outdoors. Many fungi and parasites enter the body through the skin.

- Do not handle any wild or feral animals.

- If you are sick, do not take Entero-Vioform (or chloramphenicol). This has potentially dangerous side effects and has been removed from the North American market.

- If you need to have an injection overseas, make sure that a disposable syringe is used.

- Do not have blood transfusions unless they are critically needed.

Chapter 9

Dealing With A New Culture

- **What Is Culture Shock?**
- **Preparing For Culture Shock**
- **Minimizing Culture Shock**
- **Avoiding Giving Offense**

WHAT IS CULTURE SHOCK?

The Nature Of Culture Shock

Culture shock is the sometimes traumatic process which people go through when they go to live in a different country. It is caused by having to adjust our existing personal habits, values and expectations to meet new contexts and conditions.

The nature of culture shock has been extensively researched, and it is now clear that the process can be divided into four main stages. While the length and intensity of each stage vary considerably depending upon the individual person and country concerned, it now seems clear that we all go through the same stages in the same order.

Incidentally, you might assume that culture shock will be worst when people move to "exotic" countries; for example, when Americans go to live in Africa. In fact, this is not the case. The evidence suggests that Americans often suffer just as intensely when they move to countries such as England. This presumably is because we expect "exotic" countries to be different from our own and so we are prepared to be surprised by everything. We are then pleased when we find that some aspects of life are similar to those at home. On the other hand, most Americans expect life in places such as England to be familiar and they are unprepared for the major differences which they find.

The Four Main Stages Of Culture Shock

The Honeymoon Stage

In this short-lived stage you have generally positive feelings towards the new country. While feeling reassured by any familiar sights or sounds, you are thrilled by almost every new experience. You think it is cute the way buses do not operate to fixed schedules and that passengers share their seats with chickens and goats.

The Hostility Stage

After a month or so the feeling of security which you brought with you from home begins to disappear. You start to be irritated by practical problems: dealing with different money, not finding certain products, etc. Language and cultural differences make you feel that local people are unfriendly and unhelpful. You now want to know why the buses cannot run on time, as they do in Chicago or Toronto, and why you should be expected to share them with livestock.

The Depression Stage

After about three months your negative feelings reach a peak and you are critical of almost everything and everyone. You may even start to exhibit some physical symptoms of stress: overeating, drinking too much, insomnia, sudden fits of crying, etc. You now spend all of your free time with other expatriates, sharing your latest horror stories about the buses and agreeing that the bus system accurately reflects the country's major political, economic, cultural and moral flaws.

The Adaptation/Acceptance Stage

After four or five months life starts to seem less bleak. You begin to appreciate "good" aspects of the new culture and to be more accepting of "bad" ones. Even if you do not like the new country as much as you had hoped, you feel confident that you can cope with it. Like all other middle class people in the country, you now travel exclusively by taxi or train, and you laugh every time you see newly-arrived foreigners struggling to deal with buses.

PREPARING FOR CULTURE SHOCK

Before You Leave Home

It is important to accept that you will inevitably suffer from culture shock when you start working abroad, because this will allow you to start preparing yourself. You cannot completely avoid culture shock but you certainly can do a lot to minimize its negative effects and to help yourself reach the Adaptation Stage sooner rather than later. If you follow the advice given below, you should be better prepared both psychologically and physically for life overseas. This should make your first months overseas more enjoyable - or at least more bearable.

1 Find out as much as you can about the country: read travel guides and books about the country's history; look at maps; read postings on the Job Information Journal pages of Dave's ESL Cafe (www.eslcafe/jobinfo/index.html).

2 Talk or correspond with people from the country or with people who have lived there. In the case of natives of the country, ask them which aspects of life in North America have been the hardest for them to adjust to. If you talk with a "foreigner" who lived there, get them to tell you what they enjoyed most and least.

3 Try to find a TV or video film about the city and area where you are going to be living. This will help to prepare you for the sights and sounds of your new home.

4   Start learning the language, even if it is a tough one or you do not
    have a gift for language learning. If you cannot find any classes,
    use a home-study course. Try to find someone who knows the
    language and can help you to practice it. Even if you do not get
    very far with your studies, knowing just a few words and phrases
    will help: you will feel less isolated when you arrive and local
    people will certainly appreciate that you have made an effort.

5   One of the causes of culture shock is living in totally unfamiliar
    surroundings. So bring with you to the new country a few
    personal items which will immediately add a touch of the familiar
    to your new home. These might include some favorite books and
    CD's, a photo album, a couple of framed pictures of your family,
    and perhaps one or two other objects which you have had for
    years.

MINIMIZING CULTURE SHOCK

When You Arrive

You cannot even start the process of adaptation as long as you are still
living out of a suitcase. So try to arrange your long-term housing as
quickly as possible after you arrive in the overseas country. Then do
everything you can to turn your new apartment or house into a home
by putting out personal items, buying and putting up inexpensive pictures or wall-hangings, etc.

Eight Simple Ways To Minimize Culture Shock

1   Establish some regular habits, such as always having coffee in
    the same cafe or buying a newspaper at the same newsstand. This
    will make you start to feel more like a resident and less like a
    tourist or outsider, and it will help to get you known to local
    traders. (In the early days of living abroad it can be very comfort-
    ing to have a few people say hello to you when you walk around
    town.)

2 Use part of every weekend to do something fun which you could not do back home: go to a museum, shop at the local outdoor market, visit a local landmark. This will help to remind you of why you came overseas and it will offset some of the problems which you will inevitably face at work or in daily life.

3 There are inevitably going to be times when you feel lonely and bored. So get a hobby, preferably one that is inexpensive and easy to indulge in. Here are just a few possibilities from among hobbies adopted by colleagues of mine in various countries: drawing, painting, playing the harmonica, birdwatching, writing poetry, knitting, and collecting local plants.

4 Keep on learning the language and reading about the country.

5 Spend time with people who know and like the country. Talk with them about problems which you are having and ask them about things which you do not understand.

6 Avoid spending too much time with expatriates who make a habit of complaining about every aspect of the country and its people.

7 Keep in regular contact with friends and family back home. This will make you feel much less isolated.

8 From your very first day in the country, keep a journal. In the front, write a list of things you do not like about life in your home country. Then, whatever else you write in the journal, be sure to mention at least one interesting or pleasant thing that you do or see every single day. When life starts getting you down, look back through your journal entries and at the list in the front.

AVOIDING GIVING OFFENSE

When you first start living in a foreign culture, it is extremely easy to offend people unintentionally, sometimes with disastrous long-term results. Let me give you a couple of actual examples of such mistakes made by expatriate teachers overseas. The examples I have chosen are fairly extreme ones but most EFL teachers can tell you of at least one similar mistake which they made when they first lived abroad.

When Roy was working in Peru, he got engaged to a local woman, who took him to have dinner with her family. During the evening he stood with his hands in his pockets, chatting with the woman's father. For months afterwards the father would hardly speak to Roy. Why? In Peru, as in many other countries, it is unbelievably rude and disrespectful to speak to an older person with your hands in your pockets!

Anne was teaching in Beirut. One day she had to explain the meaning of "to march." She clarified the word by miming a US soldier marching across the classroom and saying "I'm marching." Then she walked normally across the room and said "In Lebanon, marching is more like this." The next day, she was informed by the director that her visa had been revoked and that she had to leave the country within 48 hours. Why? One of her students told his uncle, a major in the army, that Anne had made fun of the Lebanese army. The uncle phoned a friend in the immigration ministry and arranged for Anne's visa to be revoked.

Appearing To Be Critical

Most reasonable people realize that it is impolite (and usually badly received) to criticize aspects of a country to natives of that country. After all, whatever reservations we may have about our own country, most of us are quick to react if a visitor criticizes it. Overseas you may find that many people are so defensive about their countries that they often read implied criticisms into what we intend as neutral comments or questions. The incident with Anne in Beirut was an example of this. I saw a similar if less dramatic example when I was observing an EFL class in San Francisco some years ago.

Barbara was teaching a group of Russian adults when the name of Shakespeare came up during class. Not knowing whether people read Shakespeare in Russia, Barbara asked a student if he had heard of Shakespeare. The student stood up, pounded his fist on his desk and said: "Yes, I know Shakespeare. Yes, I have read Shakespeare. I read 'Hamlet' and 'Macbeth' and 'King Lear.' Have you read 'King Lear'? I have read Byron. Have you read Byron? We have libraries in Russia, and museums, and schools, and universities. And they are all free, not like in the United States." Then he sat down again, leaving Barbara absolutely stunned.

So at least until you know local people quite well, try to avoid saying things like: "I haven't seen many movie theaters," "Most cars here seem to be older than in the USA" or "Do you have any museums?" However innocent your intentions, people may well assume that you are criticizing their country and drawing unfavorable comparisons with your country.

Avoiding Political Problems

When working abroad, it is very important to avoid saying anything that can be seen as a criticism of the local government, the political system, the military or the state religion. Many foreign countries are not democracies and virtually none have any tradition of free speech. So any comments on the topics mentioned above may offend people and may even be illegal. I knew a teacher in Argentina who had serious problems because he called the Falkland Islands by their English name instead of the "Malvinas." More recently, I heard of an American teacher in Thailand who caused great offense to his students by mentioning the movie "The King and I," which Thais strongly feel paints a very unfavorable picture of their country.

In this context, it is particularly important that you find out which topics cannot safely be discussed in class. In many countries you are likely to discover that it would be unacceptable to have discussions on most interesting topics, including anything relating to politics or sex.

Avoiding Offensive Gestures

As well as being careful of what you say, you need to be careful about your gestures, body language and physical behavior. Many common gestures and actions which may be acceptable in Canada or the USA are regarded as impolite or offensive overseas. Any good travel or cultural guide will point out which gestures and behaviors you should avoid in specific countries.

The following list highlights just some of the actions which can cause problems for North Americans living overseas:

* Blowing or wiping your nose in front of other people is impolite in countries from Japan to Belgium.

* An ¨OK¨ sign formed by using your thumb and index finger is a very rude sign in Singapore, Russia, etc.

* Crossing your legs with an ankle on your knee is offensive in countries from France to China.

* For a woman to sit with legs crossed is very impolite or even obscene in all Muslim countries and in many others.

* For a man or woman to sit with knees far apart is offensive in most countries, including many in Europe and Latin America.

* Wearing a hat or cap indoors is extremely rude in most countries.

* Wearing shoes in people's homes is offensive in most Asian countries.

* Speaking to someone with your hands in your pockets or on your hips is almost universally rude and insulting.

* Sitting on or leaning against desks or tables is very impolite in many Asian countries, including Japan.

* Putting your feet on seats in buses or trains is offensive almost everywhere, including European countries such as England.

* Chewing gum will offend people in most countries. In Singapore, it will even earn you a hefty fine.

* Eating or drinking in the street or in class is regarded as impolite just about everywhere overseas.

* Talking loudly in public (including on buses and in restaurants) is offensive in most countries.

Chapter 10

Your First Weeks Overseas

- **Adjusting To Your Teaching Job**
- **Finding Out What Your Students Like**
- **Behaving Appropriately Outside Of Class**

ADJUSTING TO YOUR TEACHING JOB

Your First Priorities As A Teacher

Unless you have a lot of previous experience of living and teaching overseas, the first few weeks in your new job are going to be pretty tough. You will have to spend time and energy on adjusting to the new culture, settling in to new housing, finding your way around town, etc. At the same time, and probably starting within a few days of your arrival, you will have to plan and teach 25-35 hours of classes per week. Inevitably, there is a danger that you will be more preoccupied with adjusting to your new living conditions than with your responsibilities at work.

It is really important to remember that work has to be your absolute top priority: it is why you were given a job, a work permit, and a residence visa. You also need to realize that first impressions at work are crucial: how your employer, your students and your colleagues view you in the first week or two may well determine how they will continue to view you throughout the period of your contract.

So for your first weeks in your new job you need to focus on:

* carrying out your teaching duties;
* gaining the respect and trust of your students;
* showing your employer that you are a responsible professional.

Twelve Specific Ways To Avoid Problems

Although this book does not attempt to deal with TEFL methodology, it may be useful here to give some advice on how best to approach your first lessons.

The twelve pieces of advice below should help you to establish the best possible relationship with your students, as well as with your employer and your colleagues. At least initially, this is much more important than having fun outside work. It is even more important than being creative with your teaching: the time for creativity is after you have established a good relationship with all of your classes.

1. Always Be Punctual

Fee-paying students, particularly adult ones, really hate any lack of punctuality on the part of a teacher. So, you need to be in your classroom before the scheduled class time. Start every lesson at exactly the scheduled time, even if not all your students are present. Also, make sure that you finish every class at exactly the scheduled time, and that you keep any coffee-breaks to the official length.

2. Look The Part

In many countries, your students' and your employer's views of you as a teacher will largely be determined by how you look. So, start by dressing fairly formally. Ask your director what he/she thinks is the most appropriate attire for teachers and try to dress like that for the first week or two.

3. Act The Part

If you do not look organized in class, students will react badly. Before each class, make sure that you: have with you all the visual aids, photocopies, etc. that you need; know how to work cassette-recorders and any other aids you intend to use; have board markers which work. In order to be organized in class, you need to arrive at school well before your scheduled teaching time.

4. Avoid Unintentionally Offending Students

Before you give your first lessons, find out which types of gestures and body language are best avoided in class; for example, whether you should stand or sit, or whether it is okay to point to students when you want them to respond.

5. Use The Textbook

Most schools base their courses on specific textbooks, which students have to buy before class. If this is the case in your school, make sure you make some use of the books in class, or at least assign sections of them for homework. If there is no set text, see whether you may choose a textbook and may ask your students to buy copies of it. Then base your classes on that book. In my experience, one of the most common of all student complaints overseas is that their teachers do not use a textbook or that they do not use the assigned text enough.

6. Research Your Teaching Points

Do not try to present, clarify or practice any language item, however apparently simple, without first researching it in a grammar book or dictionary. Also, if you are going to give students a language exercise, make sure that you have researched all of the answers. Students are sure to notice any language analysis mistakes that you make, and they will quickly lose faith in you as a teacher.

7. Plan Your Lessons

The only way to produce an effective lesson is to draw up a written plan in advance, and then to consult it during your lesson. Having a plan with you in class will also show students that you are a serious teacher.

In class, one major problem that you will certainly face is that of grading your language: speaking simply so that students of all levels can understand you. (Even fairly high level EFL students will be lost if you speak to them in the same way you would speak to other North Americans.) Until you have adjusted to your classes, the best way to deal with the language grading problem is to think through in advance what you intend to say in each lesson, and to note down on your lesson plan the actual words which you intend to use when giving explanations, instructions, etc.

8. Present Your Materials Well

Nothing makes an EFL teacher look more unprofessional than boardwork or worksheets which are badly written or misspelled. So make sure that your boardwork is neat and accurate; if necessary, practice writing on the board before your first classes. And check that any worksheets which you give students are well-presented, accurate and free from mistakes.

9. Be Organized

Students expect you to keep the class organized and to make sure that all students behave reasonably during class. You will find this is very hard to do unless you know the students' names; this is even more true with children and adolescents than with adults. So, learn your students' names quickly, or get them to put name cards on their desks. This will enable you to nominate specific students to answer questions. (A sure way to make classes seem chaotic is to ask open questions and to allow everyone to shout out answers at the same time.)

10. Keep Quiet About Your Lack Of Experience

If you are a new teacher, never tell students that this is your first teaching position. (If they ask, fudge the issue by telling them that you have done tutoring, private classes, etc.) If you did a TEFL training course, mention this and the fact that it included practice teaching. If the course was a 4-week intensive one, it is usually best not to mention how short it was; or you should express it in terms of number of hours rather than number of weeks!

11. Avoid The Word "Fun"

A lot of North Americans seem to feel it is important that all class-room activities be "fun." You should realize that this view is not shared by most overseas EFL students. Of course the latter will appreciate doing interesting and enjoyable activities in class; but this is not one of their first priorities. Learning English is a very serious (and a very expensive) matter, and your students' futures may well depend upon their success with it. So remember to introduce classroom activities by saying that they are useful or interesting, and not by labeling them as being "fun."

12. Observe Some Classes

If possible, arrange to observe some classes given by an experienced teacher in your new school before you plan or teach any lessons of your own. Two or three hours spent watching an effective teacher with local experience will give you a good idea of what will work and what will probably not work with your classes.

FINDING OUT WHAT YOUR STUDENTS LIKE

Your students may be totally unfamiliar with many of the techniques, activities, etc. which you want to use in your classes. In order to avoid problems, find out from an experienced teacher or your Director of Studies which activities most of your students are likely to know, to enjoy, to dislike, etc.

The questions below are all useful ones to ask, and they will probably prompt you to think of additional questions of your own:

- How much do the students expect to work from a textbook?

- What is their attitude towards doing written exercises in class?

- How often do they expect teachers to assign homework?

- Do they like oral drills (such as repetition drills)?

- Do they enjoy and value spelling tests and dictation?

- How do they feel about learning and repeating dialogs?

- Do they like doing role plays? If so, would they rather do them sitting at their desks or standing in front of the class?

- Do they like closed pairwork? Are they used to it? Does it matter who works with whom in pairwork?

- Do they think games and songs are useful classroom activities?

- Do they like their oral mistakes to be corrected?

- Are they prepared to talk during open class discussions?

- In free speaking work, what topics should be avoided?

- Do students like/expect teachers to use grammar terminology? Do they understand it?

- What is the school's policy on teachers using the students' language in class? How do students feel about this?

BEHAVING APPROPRIATELY OUTSIDE OF CLASS

A Different Life/Work Distinction

Those of us who live in Canada or the USA see a very clear distinction between our work and the rest of our life. While our employers may largely control what we do at work, we generally feel that they have no right to interfere with how we spend our time outside working hours. For example, we would be outraged if our boss complained about the fact that we had a little too much to drink on the weekend, or that we had a pretty noisy party at our house on Saturday night.

Unfortunately, in most countries where you may work overseas, you will find that the life/work distinction does not apply in the same way or to the same extent. Unless you work in a big city in Europe, you are likely to find that your overseas employer feels that what you do outside of work is at least partly his or her concern. Let me show you what I mean by giving some examples of problems encountered by colleagues of mine in various countries.

Bill was an American who worked in an EFL school in Istanbul, Turkey. One evening after work, in a bar a very long way from the school, he had a couple too many drinks and he got into a heated argument with some other Americans. When he arrived at school the next day, the director took Bill aside and complained about his behavior the previous evening. The director made it clear that any repetition of this behavior would lead to Bill's losing his job.

Lisa was an Irish teacher working in Prato, a small town in Italy. She went to the movies with another (male) teacher, and he ended up spending the night in her apartment. When she went to work the following afternoon, the school's director of studies warned her that she would have to be more discreet in the future, if she wanted to keep her job. The parents of one of her adolescent students had seen the male teacher leaving her apartment early that morning. They had called the school to complain about her "immoral behavior" and to ask for their son to be transferred to a different class.

Johanna was in Pusan, South Korea. Like many foreign EFL teachers in Asia, she lived in an apartment provided by her school. One holiday weekend, she threw a party which lasted until about two o'clock in the morning. It was a pretty small party and, in her view, not very noisy. Back at work, her director told her that she would lose her apartment and probably her job as well if she gave any more rowdy all-night parties.

The Reasons For Employers' Attitudes

Your relationship to your employer overseas is entirely different than that to an employer in your home country. When you get a TEFL job abroad, your school normally has to arrange for you to receive a work permit and a residence visa. In many countries, this means that the school is taking legal responsibility for you during your period of employment. It also often means that the school is expected to ensure that you do not disregard local customs and sensibilities both in and outside of work. Inevitably, therefore, schools will tend to worry about how you act even on your own time. This attitude may be difficult for North Americans to understand and accept, but it is very widespread and you will have to come to terms with it to some extent. We will look at some ways of doing so later in this chapter.

There are six major points to take into account when trying to describe and understand the attitudes of overseas employers to the out-of-school behavior of expatriate teachers:

1 As a foreigner living abroad, you will inevitably be a source of great curiosity to most local people. In many cases, you may be the first foreigner that these people have really had a chance of observing up close. So everything you do will tend to be the subject of interest and discussion.

2 Whether you want to or not, and irrespective of how you dress or behave, you will usually stand out very visibly as being a foreigner. This will be particularly true in smaller towns and cities, of course. However, it will still be true to some extent if you live in a large city in, for example, Western Europe.

3 As a teacher, you will probably have direct contact with up to a hundred students during an average working week. Each of those students will talk about you and point you out on the street to several of their friends and family members. You will also be known, at least by sight, to most or all of the other students in your school. So you can forget any idea of being able to move around, in school or outside of it, in anonymity. Wherever you go in the town where you live, and probably in surrounding areas, someone is going to recognize you as one of the foreign teachers at the such-and-such school.

4 In most countries, you will start off by being held in high regard simply because you are a teacher. However, the respect which you automatically receive through your job comes with a price tag: you will be expected to behave as local teachers are expected

to behave. In a sense, you will be held to a higher standard of behavior than other people, and anything you do which local people think is inappropriate behavior for a teacher will certainly be noticed and commented on.

5   As a foreigner, you will find that local people will tend to be very hospitable and quite tolerant when you first start living in their country. They realize that their customs are different than those in your country, and that it will take you a while to adjust. But they will expect you to adjust, and to do so within a fairly short time; if you do not, they will quickly become less hospitable and much less tolerant.

6   Every overseas employment contract which you sign is almost sure to contain some type of "good behavior" clause. This will say something to the effect that you may be dismissed from your job for any behavior which is likely, in the opinion of the employer, to harm the reputation of the organization for which you are working. Employers do not like to invoke such clauses, but they will certainly do so if your behavior offends too many local people and causes too many complaints.

Dealing With Local Attitudes

By now you are probably starting to wonder whether working and living overseas is worth all the problems and adjustments which are involved. Of course it is! I have worked in several countries, from France and Spain to Lebanon and Libya, and I have enjoyed all of them. If you are a reasonable person and behave in a responsible way, you will usually have no serious problems either in or outside of work. What is important is that you behave with some discretion until you have had time to understand local customs and expectations.

In my view, one of the keys to adapting to living abroad is to realize that people in most countries are frequently much more worried about appearances than about reality. They tend to be upset by inappropriate behavior only when it takes place in public. This is because public breaches of acceptable behavior show a blatant disregard for the local culture and laws, and local people will "lose face" if they tolerate them. I have found that in most countries, if you are careful about what you do and say in public situations, you can behave largely as you want in private.

To show you how appearances can be regarded as more important than reality, let me finish this chapter with an example from my time as a school director in Libya. This example happens to be from a Muslim country but the same attitude prevails in many parts of the world.

Most of the unmarried teachers in my school wanted to share houses with other unmarried teachers of the opposite gender. This was strictly forbidden by Libyan law, and landlords would refuse to rent houses to pairs of unmarried teachers. So whenever new teachers wanted to share a house, I advised them to say that they were related to each other: brother and sister, cousins, etc. They never had to sign anything to this effect or to prove their relationship; a spoken statement was enough to get them a lease. Was this deceitful? Not really. Why? Because none of the landlords were ever misled by what we told them; they all knew perfectly well what the real situation was. However, the family relationship fiction allowed them to turn a blind eye to what was happening. So if anyone complained that they were encouraging immorality, they could say: "It is all right. Julie is Steve's cousin. It is good that they are living together because he can make sure she is not bothered by other men."

Appendix 1

TEFL Certificate Programs

- TEFL Certificate Programs in Canada
- TEFL Certificate Programs in the USA
- TEFL Certificate Programs Abroad
- Distance Learning TEFL Certificate Programs

TEFL CERTIFICATE PROGRAMS IN CANADA

Cambridge CELTA Centers

You can find a full list of currently approved Canadian centers on the Cambridge website (www.cambridge-efl.org).

International Language Institute
       7071 Bayers Road, Halifax, Nova Scotia, B3J 1A1
       Tel: (902) 429-3636   Website: www.ili.ca
Kwantlen University College
       12666 72nd Ave., Surrey, Vancouver, BC, V3W 2M8
       Tel: (604) 599-2693
       Website: www.kwantlen.bc.ca/esl/CELTA.htm
Language Studies Canada
       124 Eglinton Ave. West, Suite 400, Toronto, Ontario,
       M4R 2G8
       Tel: (416) 488-2200
       Website: www.lsc-canada.com

Language Studies International
        1055 Yonge Street, Suite 1152, Toronto, ON, M4W 2L2
        Tel: (416) 928-6888   Website: www.lsi-canada.com

Canadian University TESOL Certificate Programs

See the "Directory of Professional Preparation Programs in TESOL
in the US & Canada" available from TESOL at:
        700 S Washington St., # 200, Alexandria, VA 22314, USA
        Tel: (703) 836-0774   Website: www.tesol.org

Other TEFL Certificate Programs in Canada

ELS International Training Centre
        105-2412 Laurel Street, Vancouver, BC, V5Z 3T2 Canada
        Tel: (604) 872-1236   Website: www.arnb.com/eslttc/
Winfield College
        201-788 Beatty Street, Vancouver, BC, V6B 2M1 Canada
        Tel: (604) 608-0538   Website: www.winfieldcollege.com
Vancouver English Centre
        840 Howe St. Ste. 200, Vancouver, BC, V6Z 2L2, Canada
        Tel: (604) 687-1600   Website: www.vec.bc.ca

TEFL CERTIFICATE PROGRAMS IN THE USA

Cambridge CELTA Centers

You can find a full list of currently approved US centers on the
Cambridge website (www.cambridge-efl.org).

Columbia Union College
        English Dept.
        7600 Flower Avenue, Takoma Park, MD 20912
        Tel: (301) 891-4059   Email: gocelta@aol.com

Embassy/CES
>330 Seventh Avenue, New York, NY 10001
>Tel: (212) 629-7300   Website: www.studygroupintl.com

International House Portland
>200 SW Market, Suite 111, Portland, OR 97201
>Tel: (503) 224-1960   Website: www.ih-usa.com

International House San Diego
>2725 Congress Street, Suite 2M, San Diego, CA 92110
>Tel: (619) 299-2339   Website: www.ih-usa.com

North Harris College Houston
>2700 WW Thorne Drive, Houston, TX 77073
>Tel: (281) 618-5604   Website: www.nhceducatesu.com

St Giles Language Teaching Center
>1 Hallidie Plaza, Ste. 350, San Francisco, CA 94102, USA
>Tel: (415) 788-3552   Website: www.stgiles-usa.com

School for International Training
>Center for Teacher Education, Training & Research,
>Kipling Road, P.O. Box 676, Brattleboro, VT 05301
>Tel: (802) 258-3350   Website: www.sit.edu/tesolcert
>**Note:** Only a few courses run by SIT are CELTA courses.

US University TESOL Certificate Programs

See the "Directory of Professional Preparation Programs in TESOL in the US & Canada," available from TESOL at:
>700 S Washington St., Suite 200, Alexandria, VA 22314, USA
>Tel: (703) 836-0774   Website: www.tesol.org

Other TEFL Certificate Programs in the USA

Boston Language Institute
>648 Beacon St., Boston, MA 02215
>Website: www.teflcertificate.com

LADO
>2233 Wisconsin Ave. NW, Washington, DC 20007, USA
>Tel: (202) 333-4222   Website: www.lado.com

Midwest ESL Institute
    19 N Pinckney Street, Madison, WI 53703-2829, USA
    Tel: (800) 765-8577   Website: mttp.com
Seattle University School of TESL
    2601 NW 56th Street, Seattle, WA 98107, USA
    Tel: (206) 781-8607
    Website: www.seattleu.edu/soe/stesl/
School for International Training
    Center for Teacher Education, Training & Research,
    Kipling Road, P.O. Box 676, Brattleboro, VT 05301
    Tel: (802) 258-3350   Website: www.sit.edu/tesolcert
Transworld Schools
    701 Sutter St., 2nd Floor, San Francisco, CA 94109, USA
    Tel: (415) 928-2835
    Website: www.transworldschools.com

TEFL CERTIFICATE PROGRAMS ABROAD

Cambridge CELTA Centers

Cambridge CELTA courses are offered in over 40 countries world-wide. You can obtain a list of all Cambridge CELTA centers by visiting the Cambridge website or from:
    Cambridge ELT,
    University of Cambridge,
    1 Hills Road,
    Cambridge CB1 2EU, England
    Tel: (1223) 553311   Fax: (1223) 553068
    Website: www.cambridge-efl.org

Trinity College TESOL Certificate Centers

You can obtain a list of Trinity TESOL Certificate centers by visiting the Trinity website or from:

Trinity College,
16 Park Crescent,
London W1N 4AP, England
Tel: (171) 323-2328   Fax: (171) 323-2328
E-mail: tesol@trinitycollege.co.uk
Website: www.trinitycollege.co.uk

Independent TEFL Programs Abroad

Some of these programs are run by organizations based in the USA
or Canada and you can obtain details of these programs from the
head offices of the organizations concerned. The full addresses are
given earlier in this Appendix.

SIT - Australia, Japan, Thailand
        Contact: School for International Training, Brattleboro, VT
Vancouver English Centre - Mexico
        Contact: Vancouver English Centre in Vancouver, Canada.

Several organizations based overseas offer TEFL certificate courses
in a variety of countries. The three organizations listed below have
been offering courses for several years:

International Training Center (ITC) - Prague & Barcelona
        Website: www.itc-training.com
TEFL International - Thailand and some other countries
        Website: www.teflintl.com
Via Lingua - Czech Republic and some other countries
        Website: www.vialingua.com

DISTANCE LEARNING TEFL CERT. PROGRAMS

The organizations listed below are just a few of those which operate
distance learning TEFL programs.

English International
> 14627 Cypress Valley Drive, Cypress, TX 77429, USA
> Website: www.english-international.com

New School
> English Language Studies Center, 68 Fifth Avenue, New York, NY 10011, USA
> Website: www.nsu.newschool.edu/english

COMBINED ONSITE & DISTANCE COURSES

Oxford Seminars, a well-established Canadian organization, offers intensive 60-hour onsite TESL/TEFL training courses in major cities across Canada and in some US cities. Participants who complete the 60-hour course can then opt to extend their training and certification by taking one or more of four 40-hour specialization modules offered via correspondence. One popular module focuses on Teaching English to Children, while another focuses on Teaching Business English. Oxford Seminars also provides its program graduates with job placement assistance.

> Oxford Seminars
> 461 Princess Street, Kingston, Ontario, K7L 1C3, Canada
> Website: www.oxfordseminars.com

Appendix 2

Some Major Resources

TEFL METHODOLOGY & LANGUAGE BOOKS

Books

You can find a list of recommended books on TEFL methodology and language development in Chapter 2 (pages 27-30).

TEFL Bookstores & Suppliers

Very few traditional bookstores carry a really good selection of EFL/ TEFL publications. However, most popular EFL/TEFL titles can be purchased on-line from Barnes and Noble (www.barnesandnoble.com) or Amazon (www.amazon.com).

Two suppliers carry an excellent range of EFL/TEFL publications. Both supply books by on-line purchase or by traditional mail order, and both produce descriptive catalogs of the titles which they carry:

ALTA Book Center
14 Aidrian Court, Burlingame, CA 94010, USA
       Tel: (800) ALTA-ESL   Fax: (800) ALTA-FAX
       E-mail: altaesl@aol.com
       Website: www.altaesl.com

DELTA Systems Co.
       1400 Miller Parkway, McHenry, IL 60050-7030, USA
       Tel: (800) 323-8270   Fax: (800) 909-9901

E-mail: via website
Website: www.delta-systems.com

English International books and videos can be purchased directly from the publisher. You can find details at the English International website (www.english-international.com).

LISTS OF OVERSEAS EMPLOYERS

The most comprehensive list of overseas TEFL employers is published on a PC disk by English International. This disk contains the addresses of more than 1400 overseas employers, including 500 employers in the EU countries of Western Europe. You can find details on the E.I. website (www.english-international.com).

TEFL JOBS WEBSITES

Worldwide Vacancies

There are many sites which claim to offer job listings from around the world but very few of them are really worth accessing. The sites listed below are the only ones which regularly carry significant listings of current job vacancies in many different regions:

www.jobs.edunet.com

www.eslcafe.com/joblist/
> This section of Dave's ESL Cafe is undoubtedly the best jobs site on the web. The ESL Cafe has a separate page for jobs in Korea (see below).

www.eslworldwide.com

www.tefl.com

www.tefl.net

The Dave's ESL Cafe website also includes a "Web Guide to Jobs" section containing many links to job search sites. Unfortunately, many of the links either do not function or else lead you to sites which carry little or no useful information.

Vacancies In Specific Countries

China: www.teach-in-china.com

Japan: www.ohayosensei.com
            www.jobsinjapan.com
            www.eltnews.com

Korea: www.eslcafe.com/jobs/korea

Thailand: www.taiteach.com

OTHER USEFUL TEFL WEBSITES

There are now scores of websites which claim to offer valuable advice and information on teaching EFL overseas. In my experience, very few of these sites contain useful material. Unless you are willing to spend a huge amount of time on-line, I would recommend that you consider accessing only the sites listed below.

www.eslcafe.com/jd/
    By far the most popular site for the discussion of issues relating to TEFL jobs and living overseas. Although a disproportionate number of postings involve complaints from American teachers in Asia, and particularly Korea, it is still worth visiting the site regularly.

www.eslcafe.com/discussion/dz1/
    A good site for the discussion of TEFL training programs. If you are thinking of doing a TEFL course, you should check out this site.

www.eslcafe.com/jobinfo/index.html
    This "Job Information Journal" contains a country-by-country collection of postings by teachers with overseas experience. Many of the postings are outdated or not very informative but some give very useful data and advice.

www.tefl.net

    This hosts discussion groups on jobs and other TEFL-related issues.

www.eflweb.com

    A number of interesting articles on teaching and living in Finland, Hungary, Japan, Korea, Spain, Taiwan and Thailand.

www.english-international.com

    I run this site, which has useful information on TEFL training programs and on the TEFL job market. However, except for details of English International publications and distance courses, most of the information on the site is also contained in this book!

www.amscan.org.work.html

    This site carries a great deal of useful information on working in Scandinavian countries.

Appendix 3

Test Your Knowledge Of English

Many people assume that all educated native speakers of English know the language well enough to teach it effectively. This is very far from the truth. To be an EFL teacher, it is not enough to speak and write English well. You also need to know a lot **about** the language, and particularly about its grammar, vocabulary, and pronunciation.

To check how much you really know about English and the way in which it operates, try taking the "test" below. It includes just a few of the questions which EFL students typically ask their teachers.

• You should allow yourself a maximum of two minutes to answer each question.
• You should complete the test without looking in a grammar book or dictionary.

There is an answer key and commentary at the end of the test.

THE TEST

1) "Big" and "large" are synonyms. So why can you say "It is a big problem" but not "It is a large problem"?

2) What is grammatically wrong with the sentence "I would like to briefly make a point"?

3) Which is the most common vowel sound in spoken English?

4)   Why can you not say "I am living here since 1990"?

5)   Which syllable is stressed in "record" and "export"?

6)   Which is correct: "If I were you" or "If I was you"?

7)   Which is the "odd word out" in the following adjectives, and why?   fat, overweight, heavy, thin, willowy, skinny

8)   What is a phrasal verb?

9)   What is the negative form of "He must leave now"?

10) How do you pronounce the letters "ed" at the end of regular past tense verbs?

11) Does the voice usually rise or fall at the end of questions?

12) Think of five ways to express "She arrived at 6:00" in the future.

13) Which is grammatically more correct: "I have just seen her" or "I just saw her"?

14) How many sounds are there in spoken English?

15) Which spelling is correct: "theater" or "theatre"?

ANSWERS TO THE TEST

1)   "Big" can be used to describe both concrete and abstract items, but "large" is normally used only to describe concrete ones.

2)   Nothing whatsoever. There is no logical reason why infinitives should not be split in English. The "rule" about not splitting them is based solely on the fact that infinitives cannot be split in Latin. There is absolutely no reason why rules of Latin grammar should be applied to English.

3)   The most commonly used vowel sound in English is the "schwa" (written phonemically as an upside down "e"). What is the schwa? It is the unstressed vowel found, for example, in the second syllable of "medal" and "children."

4) "Since" does not refer only to present time; it refers to a period of time starting in the past and continuing into the present. So the verb tense in the sentence needs to be one which also relates to both the past and the present. The sentence needs to be rephrased using the Present Perfect Simple or Progressive: "I have lived / I have been living here since 1990."

5) It depends on whether you are using the words as nouns or verbs. As nouns, "a record" and "an export" have stress on the first syllable. The verbs "to record" and "to export" have stress on the second syllable.

6) Older, prescriptive grammar books insist on the use of the subjunctive form "were." Most modern, descriptive grammar books accept both "were" and "was" as being grammatically acceptable, but they suggest that "If I were" still is more appropriate in formal contexts.

7) The odd word out is "willowy." The other words refer only to weight. "Willowy" refers to a combination of weight and height. (Someone cannot be short and willowy, for example.)

8) It is a phrase made up of a verb and one or more prepositions (or adverbs). The meaning of the whole phrase cannot be deduced from the component words. For example, you may understand the words "run" and "across" but still not understand the sentence "He ran across a friend."

9) It depends upon what meaning you are trying to convey. In the sense of something not being permitted, the negative form is either "must not" or (more commonly in American English) "cannot." In the sense of something not being compulsory, the negative form is "does not have to."

10) There are three possible pronunciations: /d/ as in "climbed," /t/ as in "walked," and /id/ as in "waited."

11) Linguists generally agree that, in both British and American English, the voice usually falls at the end of questions which begin with question words ("Where," "When," etc.). The voice normally rises at the end of questions which start with auxiliary verbs ("Have," "Did," etc.). However, particularly

in American English, many people now use rising intonation at the end of most questions.

12) "She will arrive at 6:00." "She arrives at 6:00." "She is arriving at 6:00." "She will be arriving at 6:00." "She is going to arrive at 6:00." "She's going to be arriving at 6:00."

13) Both are equally correct in American English. "I just saw her" is not correct in British English.

14) Most speakers of American English use a total of 42-43 consonants, vowels and diphthongs. (Most British speakers use a total of 44 sounds.) Of course, exactly which sounds you use will depend upon which regional accent you have.

15) Both spellings are equally correct in American English, although "theater" is now more commonly used. In British and Canadian English, only "theatre" is correct.

HOW DID YOU DO ON THE TEST?

If you answered 13-15 of the questions correctly, you already have a very good knowledge of English.

If you answered 10-12 of the questions correctly, you did well but you need to brush up on your knowledge of English a little.

If you answered fewer than 10 questions correctly, you definitely need to improve your formal knowledge of English before starting to teach EFL.

Appendix 4

International Programs & Employers

- Introduction
- Organizations Based In North America
- Organizations Based In Europe

INTRODUCTION

Most EFL schools, programs and agencies offer jobs only within one country. Contact details for these can be found in Appendix 5.

However, some organizations recruit teachers for jobs in a variety of countries. Details of these organizations are given below.

ORGANIZATIONS BASED IN NORTH AMERICA

Organizations Which Recruit Credentialed Teachers

People who are qualified and credentialed as public school teachers are eligible for most positions which are available with EFL schools. However, they are also eligible for positions teaching EFL or other subjects in international elementary and high schools. The positions offer excellent salaries, benefits and working conditions. Teachers who are interested in them should contact the following organizations:

Education Information Services (EIS), P O Box 620662, Newton, MA 02162-0662, USA
Tel: (781) 433-0125   Fax: (781) 237-2842

University of Northern Iowa, Overseas Placement Service for Educators, UNI, Cedar Falls, Iowa 50614-0390, USA

Tel: (319) 273-2083.   Fax: (319) 273-6998
E-mail: overseas.placement@uni.edu
Website: www.uni.edu/placemnt/student/internat.html

ISS, Education Staffing, 15 Roszel Road, P O Box 5910,
Princeton, NJ 08543, USA
Tel: (609) 452-0990   Fax: (609) 452-2690
E-mail: iss@iss.edu
Website: www.iss.edu

Other Organizations

A large number of TEFL jobs are available in binational centers or
other institutes supported by the US government. Recruitment for these
schools is carried out by the individual centers, the addresses of which
are included in the country-by-country lists in Appendix 5.

Many TEFL positions overseas are available through the Peace Corps.
These positions, which are open only to US citizens, often provide
better salaries and working conditions than other TEFL jobs in the
countries concerned. Previous TEFL training is not essential, but there
is fierce competition for appointments. Details of the Peace Corps
TEFL program can be obtained from:

Peace Corps, 1111 20th St. NW, Washington, DC 20526, USA
Tel: (800) 424-8580
Website: www.peacecorps.gov

Qualified EFL teachers who want to teach in the smaller countries of
Central or Eastern Europe can apply to the SOROS Foundation, which
offers positions with comparatively good salaries and conditions in
countries such as Azerbaijan, Bulgaria, Kazakhstan, Romania and
Uzbekistan. Preference is given to teachers with an MA TESOL, but
some positions are open to teachers with a TEFL certificate and teaching experience. Full details can be obtained from:

SPELT, Univ. of Montana, Linguistics Program, Missoula, MT
59812, USA
Tel: (406) 243-5164.
E-mail: soros@selway.umt.edu

A very limited number of TEFL jobs in Asia are available through the
YMCA. Teachers who are interested should contact:

YMCA Overseas Service Corps, 101 North Wacker Drive, Chicago, IL 60606, USA
Tel: (800) 872-9622   Fax: (312) 977-9036.

Teachers who want to work in North Africa or the Mid East should contact some of the organizations listed in Appendix 5.

Berlitz, which has over 350 branches or affiliates, has a mixed reputation as an employer but it is well established and offers many job opportunities for untrained teachers. Recruitment is carried out by the individual schools, whose addresses can be obtained from:
Berlitz Inc., 400 Alexander Park Drive, Princeton, NJ 08540-6306, USA
Tel: (609) 514-9650   Fax: (609) 514-9672
Website: www.berlitz.com

The ELS Language Centers group provides a range of good TEFL jobs in its schools in Asia, Latin America and the Mid East. Most ELS schools carry out their own recruitment but some hiring is handled by the group's head office. These jobs are advertised on the organization's website (www.els.com/home/home.html). ELS can be contacted at:
ELS Corporate Offices, 400 Alexander Park, Suite 55, Princeton, NJ 08540-6306, USA
Fax: (609) 514-3414
E-mail: info@els.com   Website: www.else.com

North Americans with TEFL training can access good jobs in various regions by applying to EF-English First. Some EF schools do their own hiring but many jobs are also available through the US recruitment office. For details of jobs and addresses of schools, contact:
EF Center, 1 Education Street, Cambridge, MA 02141, USA
E-mail: careers@ef.com   Website: www.englishfirst.com

Two Canadian organizations currently recruit for schools in Asia. One is the Canadian Institute for Teaching Overseas - CITO, which can be contacted at:
CITO, 57 Mayflower Dr., New Glasgow, Nova Scotia, B2H 5S3 Canada
Tel: (902) 752-3678   Fax: (902) 752-4066
E-mail: cito@north.nsis.com
Website: www.nsis.com/~cito/CITO.html

The other organization is Goal Recruiting, which sends teachers to Taiwan, Korea and Thailand. You can contact Goal Recruiting at:
307 Glebemont Ave., Toronto, Ontario, M4C 3V3 Canada
Tel: (416) 696-2344
E-mail: apply@goalasia.com
Website: www.goalasia.com

Programs & Recruitment Organizations Which Require A Fee

Although trained teachers should not need to pay any type of fee to obtain an overseas job, untrained teachers may want to consider obtaining a job through one of the following organizations, all of which charge some type of fee:

English for Everybody, 655 Powell St., Suite 505, San Francisco, CA 94108, USA
Tel: (415) 789-7641

Alliances Abroad, 409 Deep Eddy Ave., Austin, TX 78703, USA
Tel: (888) 6-ABROAD
E-mail: info@alliancesabroad.com
Website: www.alliancesabroad.com/alliances

Taking Off, P O Box 104, Newton Highlands, MA 02161, USA
Tel: (617) 630-1606   Fax: (617) 630-1605
E-mail: Takingoff@aol.com

The World University Service of Canada places Canadian teachers in a range of Asian countries, including Laos and Vietnam:
World University Service of Canada, 1404 Scott St., P O Box 3000, Ottawa, Ontario, Canada
Fax: (613) 798-0990
E-mail: recruit@wusc.ca

Several US universities and other related organizations place university students or graduates as teaching assistants in schools abroad. A list of programs, many of which charge a substantial placement fee, can be found at the University of Michigan website (www.umich.edu/~icenter/overseas/work/teach_no_cert2.html). Details of some of the better known programs are given below.

WorldTeach sends hundreds of volunteers a year to Asia, Latin America and Africa. The volunteers receive airfare, accommodations and a good monthly stipend but they pay a program fee of about $4000. Contact:
WorldTeach Inc., Harvard Institute for International Development, 14 Story Street, Cambridge, MA 02138, USA
Tel: (800) 4-TEACH-0   Fax: (617) 495-1599
E-mail: info@worldteach.org
Website: www.worldteach.org

The American Slavic Student Internship Service Training Corporation (ASSIST) offers placements in Russia, the Czech Republic, Slovakia and Latvia. Airfare, housing and a stipend are provided. The program fees vary but are usually $4000 or more. Contact:
ASSIST, 1535 SW Upper Hall, Portland, OR 97201, USA
E-mail: assistusa@aol.com

The Central European Teaching Program places college graduates in schools in Central/Eastern European countries. Participants pay a fee of $1000 and receive placement with housing and salary. Contact:
CETP, Beloit College, 700 College Street, Beloit,WI 53511, USA
Fax: (608) 363-2449
E-mail: dunlop@beloit.edu
Website: www.beloit.edu/~cetp

The InterExchange program places college graduates for one year in schools in the Czech Republic, Bulgaria, Hungary and Poland. The participants usually receive housing and a stipend, but not airfare or health insurance. The program fee is in the $300-$500 range. Contact:
InterExchange, 161 Sixth Avenue, New York, NY 10013, USA
Fax: (212) 924-0575
E-mail: interex@earthhlink.net
Website: www.interexchange.org

ORGANIZATIONS BASED IN EUROPE

UK-Based Organizations

The British Council has institutes in many countries. Recruitment for teaching positions is carried out locally by the overseas institutes. These offer good salaries and conditions, but they require all teachers to

137

have a recognized TEFL certificate, such as the CELTA or the Trinity TESOL. The addresses of all Council institutes can be obtained from: The British Council, The British Embassy, 3100 Massachusetts Ave. NW, Washington, DC 20008-3600, USA
Tel: (202) 588-6500   Fax: (202) 588-7918
E-mail: enquiries@britishcouncil-usa.com
Website: www.britishcouncil-usa.org

The British Council, 80 Elgin St., Ottawa, Ontario, K1P 5K7 Canada
Tel: (613) 237-1530   Fax: (613) 569-1478
Website: www.britcoun.org/canada/

The British Council, 1000 ouest rue de La Gauchetiere, Bureau 4200, Montreal, Quebec, H3B 4Q5 Canada
Tel: (514) 866-5863   Fax: (514) 866-5322
E-mail: britcnl@alcor.concordia.ca

The UK-based International House organization has more than 100 affiliated schools in 30 countries. The schools generally offer above average salaries and working conditions, together with opportunities for teacher development. However, IH schools employ only teachers with the RSA/Cambridge CELTA. Some recruitment is carried out by the IH Staffing Unit in England, and this requires applicants to be interviewed in London. Contact:
Recruitment Unit, IH, 106 Piccadilly, London W1V 9FL, UK
Tel: (171) 491 2598   Fax: (171) 499 3708
E-mail: worldrecruit@ihlondon.co.uk
Website: www.ihworld.com
Recruitment is also undertaken by the individual IH schools, some of which will appoint North American teachers after a satisfactory phone interview. The addresses of all IH schools are on the group's website.

Another large UK-based organization is Language Link, which has 100 schools in Central and Eastern Europe, Vietnam and China. Like most other British EFL organizations, Language Link recruits only teachers with recognized TEFL training and certification. The group prefers to employ teachers who hold the CELTA or the Trinity College TESOL, but it will consider applications from teachers with other TEFL certificates. You can get full details from:
Language Link, 21 Harrington Rd., London SW7 3EU, England

Tel: (171) 225 1065.
E-mail address: info@language.ru
Website: www.language.ru/e/jobs/

The Bell Educational Trust offers very good conditions of work in a dozen branches and affiliates in Europe and Thailand. Applicants must have at least a recognized TEFL certificate (CELTA or Trinity TESOL), and they usually have to be willing to attend interviews in the UK. For information on current vacancies, contact:
Bell Language Schools, Overseas Dept., Hillcross, Red Cross Lane, Cambridge CB2 2QX, England
Tel: (1223) 212333   Fax: (1223) 410282
Website: www.bell-centres.com

In addition to jobs with the school groups mentioned above, many positions are available through UK-based recruitment agencies. All of these agencies require teachers to have a TEFL certificate, preferably the CELTA or the Trinity TESOL. Although there is no placement fee, applicants are usually expected to attend interviews held in England.

Most of these agencies seem to prefer British teachers, but one which is happy to consider North Americans is Saxoncourt Recruitment, which places teachers in 20 countries. Contact:
Saxoncourt Recruitment, 59 South Molton Street, London W1Y 1HH, UK
Tel: (171) 491 1919   Fax: (171) 499 3657
E-mail: recruit@saxoncourt.com
Website: www.saxoncourt.com

Some other reputable UK-based recruitment organizations are:
English Worldwide, The Italian Building, Dockhead, London SE1 2BS, UK
Tel: (171) 252 1402   Fax: (171) 231 8002
E-mail: info.eww@pop3.hiway.co.uk

Centre for British Teachers, International Recruitment, 1 The Chambers, East Street, Reading, RG1 4JD, UK
Fax: (118) 952 3924
Email: Intrecruit@cfbt-hq.org.uk
Website: www.cfbt.com

ELT Banbury, 49 Oxford Rd., Banbury, Oxon, OX16 9AH, UK

Tel: (1295) 263480   Fax: (1295) 271658
Website: www.elt-banbury.com

Other European-Based Organizations

Some other European organizations which have large numbers of branches or affiliated schools throughout the world are listed below. It should be noted that although some recruitment may be carried out by the organizations' head offices, the bulk of recruitment is handled by the individual schools overseas. The websites below carry details of some current vacancies as well as addresses of all overseas schools:

inlingua International
Website: www.inlingua.com/evaluation/main.asp

Linguarama
Website: www.linguarama.com

Wall Street Institute International
Website: www.wallstreetinstitute.com

Benedict Schools, Box 270, rue des Terreaux 29, 1000 Lausanne 9, Switzerland
Tel: 323 66 55   Fax: 311 02 29
Website: www. benedict-schools.com

Programs & Recruitment Organizations Which Require A Fee

The International Placement Group (IPG), which is based in Prague, places teachers in private language schools in Central and Eastern Europe and in Latin America. You can contact the group at:

IPG, Jezkova 9, 130 00 Prague 3, Czech Republic
Fax: (420 2) 748 067
E-mail: ipgcz@mbox.vol.cz

Appendix 5

Employers & Agents

HOW THE LIST IS ORGANIZED

The list is divided into six major sections:

- Africa (including North Africa)
- Asia
- Europe (Non-EU countries)
- Europe (EU countries)
- Latin America
- The Mid East & Turkey.

How Each Section Is Organized

Each section begins with a brief overview of the regional job market for foreign TEFL teachers. This is followed by a country-by-country listing of employers and recruitment agencies.

The countries are listed alphabetically, and countries which do not offer job possibilities have been omitted.

The Country-By-Country Lists

The international telephone dialing code is shown in bold type next to the name of each country.

Within each country, the list of overseas employers follows details of any relevant recruitment offices located in Canada or the USA.

Wherever possible, each school's listing includes the school's full postal address, together with its telephone and fax numbers and its e-mail address.

Telephone and fax numbers are preceded by the city/region code, which is given in parentheses. It should be noted that the telephone and fax numbers are normally shown in the format used in the individual overseas countries, which may not be the same as the format used in Canada and the USA.

If the location of a school is not obvious from its postal address, the city or town has been given in parentheses next to the name of the school.

Schools which are marked with a single asterisk normally recruit only teachers who are trained and/or experienced.

Schools which are marked with two asterisks are binational centers or other institutes which receive support from the US Department of State.

AFRICA (including North Africa)

Sub-Saharan Africa

It is extremely difficult to find TEFL jobs in sub-Saharan Africa. It is also virtually impossible for teachers to arrange jobs in advance from the USA or Canada unless they apply through aid organizations (such as the Peace Corps) which send teachers to the region.

One organization, IFESH-Teachers for Africa, specializes in sending qualified EFL teachers and other professional educators to the region. For more information on this program, which is open to US citizens and permanent residents, you should contact Cap Dean at IFESH-Teachers for Africa, 5040 E. Shea Blvd., Suite 260, Phoenix, AZ 85254, USA. Tel: (480) 443-1800. Fax: (480) 443-1824. E-mail: capdean@primenet.com Website: www.ifesh.org

Unless you apply through organizations such as the Peace Corps and IFESH, you are almost certainly going to have to travel to Africa to find work there. The few jobs which you may find will usually offer low salaries, permitting only a very modest lifestyle and no savings. As a rule, employers offer few benefits and do not provide housing.

It should be noted that many countries in the area suffer from high rates of both crime and disease. In addition, some of them tend to be politically and economically unstable.

North Africa

Twenty or thirty years ago, North Africa was a good TEFL market for new teachers. Unfortunately, this market has been drastically reduced in size and attractiveness by political and economic changes. Libya is currently off limits to North Americans, and Algeria is now one of the most dangerous countries in the world for Westerners. Egypt has a number of good TEFL employers, but foreigners there have been the targets of Muslim extremist groups several times over the past few years. Morocco is comparatively safe and stable, and it has a small but thriving TEFL market. Tunisia is also safe and stable, but it offers very few TEFL possibilities.

Although most TEFL jobs in North Africa have to be arranged on the spot, a few positions in Egypt, Morocco and Tunisia can be arranged in advance through Amideast, a nonprofit organization with links to the US Department of State: Amideast, 1730 M Street NW, Suite 1100, Washington, DC 20035, USA. Fax: (202) 776-7000. E-mail: inquiries@amideast.org Website: www.amideast.org

All North African countries are fascinating in terms of culture, history and geography. Teachers can generally expect to enjoy a comfortable lifestyle, although they frequently have to face problems caused by inefficient bureaucracies, erratic utilities or other services, and a very limited range of accessible entertainments and leisure activities.

Most employers offer reasonable working conditions and will assist teachers to find accommodations, but salaries are low in international terms and they rarely allow savings of more than $100-$200 a month. With the exception of positions arranged in advance through Amideast, teachers are usually responsible for paying their own airfares.

Benin   229

American Cultural Center
        B P 2012, Cotonou, Benin
        Tel: 30-45-53   Fax: 30-14-39
        E-mail: vreeland@micronet.net

Burkina Faso   226

American Language Center
        01 B P 539, Ouagadougou - 01, Burkina Faso
        Tel: 30-63-60   Fax: 31-52-73
        E-mail: alcouaga@fasonet.bf

Chad   235

English Language Program
        B P 3, N'Djamena, Chad
        Tel: 51-73-91   Fax: 51-88-31

Congo 243

CALI

B P 8622, Kinshasa 1, Zaire, Congo Democratic Republic
Tel: 88-43979   Fax: 88-46592

Egypt 20

Egypt has long been an attactive destination for EFL teachers, mainly because of the country's wealth of archaeological and historical sites. Unfortunately, the political situation is extremely unsettled at present and so teachers who are considering working there should keep themselves fully informed of recent developments.

The only cities with job openings for foreigners are Alexandria and Cairo, which offer reasonable employment opportunities, particularly for teachers with TEFL training. Salaries allow a fairly comfortable lifestyle but teachers can rarely save more than $200 or $300 a month.

Schools normally employ only teachers who are already in Egypt and they normally will not reimburse travel costs or provide housing.

Amideast English Teaching Program
3 El Pharana St., Alexandria, Egypt
Tel: (3) 483-1922   Fax: (3) 483-9644
* The British Council
9 Batalsa Street Bab Shark, Alexandria, Egypt
Tel: (3) 482-0199   Fax: (3) 484-6630
E-mail: bc.alexandria@eg.britcoun.org
* The British Council
192 Sharia El Nil, Agouza, Cairo, Egypt
Tel: (2) 303-1514   Fax: (2) 344-3076
E-mail: British.Council@eg.britcoun.org
ELS International
51 Al Shahid Abdel Moneim Hafez Street, Heliopolis, Cairo, Egypt
Tel: (2) 290-8424   Fax: (2) 419-2443
E-mail: info@els.com.eg

* ILI International House
  Mohamed Bayoumi St., Off Merghany St., Heliopolis,
  Cairo, Egypt
  Tel: (2) 291-9295   Fax: (2) 415-1082
  E-mail: ili@ritsec3.com.eg
* ILI International House
  P O Box 13, Embaba, Cairo, Egypt
  Tel: (2) 346-3087   Fax: (2) 303-5624
  E-mail: ili@starnet.co.eg

Kenya   254

American Universities Preparation & Learning Center
  Box 14842, (Chiromo La., Westlands Rd.), Nairobi, Kenya
  Tel: (2) 741-764   Fax: (2) 741-690
The Language Center
  P O 40661, (Ndemi Close, Off Ngong Rd.), Nairobi, Kenya
  Tel: (2) 569-531   Fax: (2) 568-207

Madagascar   261

English Teaching Program
  4 Lalana Dr., Razafindratandra Ambohidahy,
  Antananarivo, Madagascar
  Tel: (2) 222-0238
  E-mail: etptana@compro.mg

Morocco   212

American Language Center
  rue des Nations-Unies, Cite Suisse, Agadir, Morocco
  Tel: (8) 82-15-89   Fax: (8) 84-82-72
  E-mail: alcagad@marocnet.net.ma
American Language Center
  1 place de la Fraternite, Casablanca, Morocco
  Tel: (2) 27-52-70   Fax: (2) 20-74-57

American Language Center
      4 Zankat Tanja, Rabat 10000, Morocco
      Tel: (7) 61-269   Fax: (7) 67-255
      E-mail: alcrabat@mtds.com
* BPEC
      74 rue Jean Jaures, Casablanca, Morocco
      Fax: (2) 29-68-61
* British Centre
      3 rue Brahim el Amraoui, Casablanca, Morocco
      Tel: (2) 26-70-19   Fax: (2) 26-70-43
      E-mail: british.centre.c@casanet.ma
* EF – English First
      20 rue du Marche, Residence Benomar, Maaris,
      Casablanca, Morocco
      Tel: (2) 25-51-74   Fax: (2) 25-51-45

Niger   227

American Cultural Center
      P O Box 11201, Niamey, Niger
      Tel: 73-29-20   Fax: 73-55-60

Senegal   221

AELP
      B P 49, Dakar, Senegal
      Tel: 21-16-34   Fax: 22-23-45

South Africa   27

South Africa has a small but growing **TEFL/TESL** market, mainly located in Capetown and Johannesburg. However, because of current work permit restrictions, there are virtually no job opportunities for teachers from Canada or the USA. Teachers who want to find work there will almost certainly have to travel to South Africa to contact employers.

Teaching English Overseas

* International House Durban
    Box 50800, Musgrave, Durban,
    4062 South Africa
    E-mail: info@ihdurban.co.za
    Website: www.ihdurban.co.za
* Language Lab - International House
    4ᵗʰ Floor, Aspern House, 54 De Korte St., Braamfontein
    2001, Johannesburg, South Africa
    Tel: (11) 339-1051   Fax: (11) 403-1759
    E-mail: langlab@icon.co.za
    Website: www.ihjohannesburg.co.za

Tanzania   255

International Languages Orientation Services
    Oysterbay, Karume Road, P O Box 6995, Dar es Salaam,
    Tanzania
    Tel: (51) 667-159   Fax: (51) 112-752
    E-mail: ilos-tz@ud.co.tz

Togo   228

Centre Culturel Americain
    Rues Pelletier et Vauban, B P 852, Lome, Togo
    Tel: 212-166   Fax: 217-794

Tunisia   216

AMIDEAST
    22 rue Al Amine Al Abbassi, Cite Jardins, 1002 Tunis,
    Tunisia
    Tel: (1) 790-559   Fax: (1) 791-913
    E-mail: tunisia@amideast.org
Bourguiba Institute of Foreign Languages
    U. of Tunis, 47 Avenue de la Liberte, 1002 Tunis, Tunisia
    Tel: (1) 282-418

ASIA

Asia offers better employment possibilities for both trained and untrained teachers of EFL than any other region of the world. However, employment possibilities and working conditions vary enormously from country to country and from employer to employer. So teachers need to research job opportunities with great care.

Because the region is so vast and varied, it is impossible to generalize about job opportunities. Therefore brief comments on each significant TEFL market are given under the heading for that country.

Cambodia   855

TEFL job opportunities are still relatively limited in Cambodia, but they are increasing at a rapid rate. In almost all cases, recruitment of foreign teachers by private language institutes is carried out locally. Salaries can be surprisingly high, and are often paid in dollars, but employers do not usually provide benefits or help with housing.

The Cambodian people are friendly and hospitable to foreigners, and the country is fascinating in terms of culture and geography, but crime is widespread and the political situation is very unstable.

* ACE
        P O Box 860, Phnom Penh, Cambodia
        Tel: (23) 724 204   Fax: (23) 426 608
The Banana Centre
        #7, 9 Street, Kapkor Market, Phnom Penh, Cambodia
        Tel: (23) 60 394
Cambodian-British Centre
        P O Box 922, Phnom Penh, Cambodia
        Tel/Fax: (23) 27 541

China   86

Although China is still a Communist country, there are many opportunities for foreign EFL teachers in public colleges/universities and in the private language schools which are now springing up in various parts of the country. Jobs are usually arranged from overseas, and employers normally provide airfare and accommodations.

Working conditions are reasonably good. Salaries are high in local terms: they permit a comfortable lifestyle but rarely allow savings of more than $200-$300 a month.

Jobs can be arranged by contacting recruitment agencies or individual employers. Jobs in public colleges and universities can also be pre-arranged by applying to Chinese consulates in Canada and the USA.

There can be few safer countries for foreigners than China, and few countries which offer more interest in terms of culture, history and geography. However, prospective teachers should bear in mind that foreign goods and entertainments can be very limited, and that most Chinese institutions still tend to be very inefficient and bureaucratic.

English Language Institute - China
P O Box 265, San Dimas, CA 91773, USA
Tel: (909) 599-6773   Fax: (909) 592-9906
ISIS
49 Thompson Hay Path, Setauket, NY 11733, USA
Tel: (516) 751-6437
E-mail: tmccoy@suffolk.lib.ny.us
New China Education Foundation
1587 Montalban Drive, San Jose, CA 95120, USA
Tel: (408) 268-0418
Delter Business Institute
44 Gao Liang Qiao XieJie, Haidian, Beijing, 100044 PR China
Tel: (10) 6223-7558   Fax: (10) 6223-9116
E-mail: bingl@public3.bta.net.cn

Nanchung Institute of Aero-Technology
Foreign Affairs Office, Nanching, Jiangxi, 330034 PR China
Fax: (791) 821-3248

* EF English First
167 Tai Juan Road, Shanghai, 200031 PR China
Tel: (21) 6415-0076   Fax: (21) 6437-6607
E-mail: efsha@npc.haplink.co.cn
ELS International
14 MinHou Rd., HeXi District, Tianjin, 300202 PR China
Tel: (22) 8383-4398   Fax: (22) 8383-1951
E-mail: els_tianjin@hotmail.com
* International House Jinan - Shanda
3 Shanda South Road, Shanda Luleng, Information C. Ltd.,
Jinan City, Shanda Province, 250100 China
E-mail: shandaih@hotmail.com

China - Hong Kong   852

First Class Languages Centre
22A Bank Tower, 351-353 King's Rd., N Point, Hong Kong
Tel: 5887-7555
Venture Language Training
1A 163 Hennessey Rd., Wan Chai, Hong Kong
Tel: 2507-4985   Fax: 2511-3798

Indonesia   62

Indonesia has long been one of the biggest and best TEFL markets in Asia, and it has been easy for foreign teachers to arrange jobs either from overseas or from within Indonesia. Until 1998, most jobs offered good salaries and working conditions, allowing teachers (particularly those outside of Jakarta) to live well, to enjoy their time in the country and to save $400-$500 a month.

Unfortunately, there has been a decline in the country's economic prosperity and political stability, and the situation is still very unsettled. It continues to be possible to arrange good jobs in advance or on the spot, but most schools now recruit only trained and/or experienced teachers. Also, foreign teachers report being very worried by recent social and political developments, and they say that inflation and devaluation have made significant savings impossible.

Although the political situation may be improving, prospective teachers should keep a very close eye on developments.

AELT Center
  Jl. R.S. Fatmawati 42A, Jakarta Selatan 12430, Indonesia
  Tel: (21) 769-1001   Fax: (21) 751-3304
* EF - English First (Head office of 19 schools in Indonesia)
  Wisma Tamara 4th Floor, Suite 402, Jl. Jend. Sudirman
  Kav. 24, Jakarta 12920, Indonesia
  Tel: (21) 520-6477   Fax: (21) 520-4719
  E-mail: recruitment@englishfirst.co.id
  Website: http://only.at/english.first
* EEC
  Jalan Let. Jend. S. Parman 68, Slipi, Jakarta 11410,
  Indonesia
  Tel: (21) 532-3176   Fax: (21) 532-3178
  E-mail: eec@vision.net.id
  Website: www.indodirect.com/eec
EEP
  Jalan Wijaya VIII / 4, Kebayoran Baru, Jakarta Selatan
  12160, Indonesia
  Tel: (21) 722-0812   Fax: (21) 720-1896
  E-mail: eepby@pacific.net.id
* EEP
  Jalan Lombok 43, Bandung 40115, Indonesia
  Tel: (22) 421-1651
ELS International
  Jl. Wijaya IX/21, Kebayoran Baru, Jakarta, Indonesia
  Tel: (21) 720-8213   Fax: (21) 720-9750
ELS International
  Jl. Dipati Ukur 89, Bandung 40132, Indonesia
  Tel: (22) 250-1293   Fax: (22) 250-2248
  E-mail: elsbdg@bdg.centrin.net.id

ELTI

Kompleks Wijaya Grand Centre, Blok F 84 A & B, Jalan
Wijaya II, Jakarta Selatan 12160, Indonesia
Tel: (21) 720-6653   Fax: (21) 720-6654

* ILP

Jl. Raya Pasar Minggu 39A, Jakarta 12780, Indonesia
Tel: (21) 798-5210   Fax: (21) 798-5212

* ILP

Jalan Jawa 34, Surabaya 60281, Jawa Timor,
Indonesia
Tel: (31) 502-3333   Fax: 931) 503-0106
E-mail: tjahjani@rad.net.id

SIT

Jalan Sunda 3, Menteng, Jakarta Pusat 10350, Indonesia
Tel: (21) 390-6920   Fax: (21) 335-671

STRIVE International

Setiabudi 1 Building, 3rd Floor / B.1, Jl. H.R. Rasuna Said,
Jakarta 12920, Indonesia
Tel: (21) 521-0690   Fax: (21) 521-0692
Website: strive@rad.net.id

YAYASAN LIA

Jl. Pramuka 30, 13120 Jakarta, Indonesia
Tel: (21) 858-3241   Fax: (21) 850-6185
E-mail: siswandi@rad.net.id

YPIA

Jl. Dr. Manur III. No. 1-A, Box 2617, Medan, 20121
Indonesia
Tel: (61) 813-197   Fax: (61) 357-140
E-mail: ppiamdn@idola.net.id

YPIA

Jl. Dharma Husada Indah Barat I, No. 3, Surabaya, 60285
Indonesia
Tel: (31) 594-7200   Fax: (31) 592-1925
E-mail: aminefsb@rad.net.id

Japan   81

In spite of recent economic problems, Japan continues to offer more good TEFL jobs for both trained and untrained teachers than any other country. Although jobs can be arranged in Japan, most teachers prefer to prearrange jobs, partly because employers generally pay airfare and provide accommodations. Applications to any of the major employers are likely to result in job offers. Teachers can also apply to individual schools but this can be very time consuming.

Although many jobs involve a heavy workload, they pay salaries which allow monthly savings of $800-$1000 or more. Teachers report that life is less stressful and much less expensive outside of the major cities of Tokyo and Osaka.

It should be noted that almost all employers insist on obtaining the necessary work permits and visas for their teachers. Because Japanese government departments move slowly, teachers may have to wait 8-12 weeks for the paperwork to be completed before they can enter Japan.

New teachers would do well to consider the large government-funded Jet Program, which offers thousands of jobs with excellent conditions of work in schools all over Japan. The JET program provides a good salary and benefits package which includes airfare, accommodations and health insurance. TEFL certification/training is preferred but not required.

AEON Inter-Cultural (200 schools throughout Japan)
    Website: www.aeonet.com
    9301 Wilshire Blvd., Suite 202, Beverly Hills, CA 90210, USA
    Tel: (310) 550-0940   Fax: (310) 550-1463
    E-mail: aeonla@aeonet.com
    203 North LaSalle St. #2100, Chicago, IL 60601, USA
    Tel: (312) 251-0900   Fax: (312) 251-0901
    E-mail: aeonchi@aeonet.com
    230 Park Avenue #1000, New York, NY 10169, USA
    Tel: (212) 808-3080   Fax: (212) 599-0340
    E-mail: aeonnyc@aeonet.com

America Eigo Gakuin (Schools throughout Japan)
P O Box 1672, St. George, UT 84771, USA
Tel: (435) 628-6301
E-mail: rpurcell@infowest.com

GEOS Language Corporation (360 schools throughout Japan)
Simpson Tower 2424, 401 Bay St., Toronto, Ontario,
Canada M5H 2YA
Tel: (416) 777-0109   Fax: (416) 777-0110
E-mail: geos@istar.ca
Website: www.twics.com/-mjm/hiring.html

Interac Nova Group (300 schools throughout Japan)
Website: www.teachinjapan.com
2 Oliver St.,, Suite 7, Boston, MA 02110, USA
Tel: (617) 542-5027   Fax: (617) 542-3115
E-mail: 74507.3070@compuserve.com
601 California, Suite 702, San Francisco, CA 94108, USA
Tel: (415) 788-3717   Fax: (415) 788-3726
E-mail: number1@nova-sf.com
1881 Yonge St., Suite 700, Toronto, Ontario, Canada M4S
3C4
Tel: (416) 481-6000   Fax: (416) 481-1362
E-mail: navacan@globalserve.net

JET Program
Office of JET Program, Japanese Embassy, 2520 Massa-
chusetts Avenue NW, Washington, DC 20008, USA
Tel: (800) INFOJET   Fax: (202) 265-9484
E-mail: eojjet@erols.com
Website: www.jet.org

Westgate Corporation
2801 W. Sepulveda Blvd., Suite 3, Torrance, CA 90505,
USA
E-mail: LorraineRF@aol.com

David English House
7-5 Nakamachi, Naka-ku, Hiroshima City, Japan
Fax: (82) 244-2651
E-mail: deh-dp@mxa.meshnet.or.jp

EC Inc.

President Bldg. 3F, West 5, South 1, Chuo-ku, Sapporo 060, Japan

Tel: (11) 221-0279   Fax: (11) 221-0248

ELS Language Center

Kobe Harborland Center Bldg. 19th Floor, 1-3-3 Higashi Kawasaki-cho, Chuo-ku, Kobe 650, Japan

Tel: (78) 371-5052   Fax: (78) 371-5054

E-mail: elskobe@po1.infosphere.or.jp

ELS Language Center

Nihon Seimei Shibuya Bldg. 8F, 1-21-1 Jinnan Shibuya-ku, Tokyo, 150-0041, Japan

Tel: (3) 5459-9686   Fax: (3) 5459-9687

E-mail: rbaker@els-japan.co.jp

ELS Language Center

Yusei Gojokai Bldg. 3F, Minami 1 Jo, Nishi 5 Chome, Chuo-ku, Sapporo 060, Japan

Tel: (11) 252-0988   Fax: (11) 252-0989

E-mail: els@tky.threewebnet.or.jp

English Club (6 schools in Saitama Province)

Naritaya Bldg. 2F, 1-3-2 Tsukagoshi, Warabi City, Saitama 335, Japan

Tel: (48) 432-7444   Fax: (48) 432-7446

GEOS Corporation

Shin Osaki Kangyo Building 4F, 6-4 Osaki 1 chome, Shinagawa-ku, Tokyo 141, Japan

Tel: (3) 5434-0200   Fax: (3) 5434-0201

E-mail: gkyomu@beehive.twics.com

Website: www.twics.com/-mjm/hiring.html

Interac Co. Ltd.

Fujibo Bldg., 2F, 2-10-28 Fujimi, Chiyoda-ku, Tokyo 102, Japan

Tel: (3) 3234-7857   Fax: (3) 3234-6055

International Education Services

Rose Hikawa Building, 22-14 Higashi 2-chome, Shibuya-ku, Tokyo 150, Japan

Tel: (3) 3498-7101   Fax: (3) 3498-7113
James English School
    Sumitomo Bldg. 9F, 20-2-6 Chuo, Aoba-ku, Sendai 980,
    Japan
    Tel: (22) 267-4911   Fax: (22) 267-4908
    E-mail: kigawa1007@aol.com
Lingo School
    11-6 Kameicho, Takamatu City, Kagawa Pref., Japan
    Tel: (878) 31-3241   Fax: (878) 31-3244
    E-mail: kyokot@kgw.enjoy.ne.jp
Trident School of Languages
    1-5-31 Imaike, Chikusa-ku, Nagoya 464, Japan
    Tel: (52) 735-1600   Fax: (52) 735-1788
Westgate Corporation (Schools throughout Japan)
    25-3 Aza Godo, Hagiwara, Gotemba, Shizuoka, 412 Japan
    Fax: (550) 89-8668
    E-mail: yukoyama@blue.ocn.ne.jp

Laos   **856**

Lao-American Language Centre
    152 Thanon Sisangvon, Ban Naxay, P O Box 327,
    Vientiane, Lao PDR
    Tel: (21) 414-321   Fax: (21) 413-760
Malaysian Management & Educational School
    311 Siamphone Rd., Ban Watnak, Km. 3, Thadeua Road,
    P O Box 4569, Vientiane, Lao PDR
    Tel: (21) 314-150   Fax: (21) 313-508
Vientiane University College
    Advanced Training Centre, That Lung Road, P O Box
    4144, Vientiane, Lao PDR
    Tel: (21) 414-873   Fax: (21) 414-346

Malaysia   **60**

Malaysia has a small but generally high quality TEFL market. Working conditions are good and teachers can live comfortably and save several hundred dollars a month. Most jobs cannot be prearranged and employers usually do not pay airfare or housing.

Bangsar English Language Centre,
    3A Jalan Telawi Tiga, Bangsar Baru, 59100 Kuala
    Lumpur, Malaysia
    Tel: (3) 555-2936   Fax: (3) 254-2408
ELS Language Center (4 schools)
    A-2-1, Wisma HB, Megan Phileo Avenue, 12 Jalan Yap
    Kwan, Seng, 50450 Kuala Lumpur, Malaysia
    Tel: (3) 266-5530   Fax: (3) 266-5220
    E-mail: clooi@els.po.my
    Website: http://els.edu.my
Institute Evergreen
    400A Jalan Pudu Raya, 55100 Kuala Lumpur, Malaysia
* International House Kuala Lumpur
    1 Jalan SS26/2, Taman Mayang Jaya, Petaling Jaya,
    Selangor Darul Ehsan, 47301 Malaysia
    E-mail: info@ih-malaysia.com
International Tuition School
    P O Box 3026, 93760 Kuching, Sarawak, Malaysia
    Tel: (82) 480-780   Fax: (82) 416-250
Ipoh Language Training Institute
    6 Jalan Tambun, Ipoh, 30350 Perak, Malaysia
    Tel: (5) 503-067   Fax: (5) 505-489
The Language House
    40 Jalan 19/3, 46300 Petaling Jaya, Malaysia
    Tel: (3) 755-0412

Mongolia   **909**

* International House Ulaanbaatar
    ESPF, Central P.O. Box 840, Ulaanbaatar, 210613
    Mongolia
    E-mail: englishteam@magicnet.mn

Nepal   977

American Language Program
GPO Box 58, Katmandu, Nepal
Tel: (1) 416 745

Pakistan   92

** Pakistan American Cultural Center
11 Fatima Jinnah Road, Karachi, Pakistan
Tel: (21) 567-0516

The Philippines   63

* The British Council
10th Floor, Taipan Place, Emerald Avenue Ortigas Business
Centre, Pasig City, Metro Manila, The Philippines
Tel: (2) 914-1011   Fax: (2) 914-1020

Singapore   65

Singapore offers an almost unique mixture of "Western" amenities
and local culture, together with an opportunity to explore other fascinating countries in the region. Although new arrivals often find the
climate tiring, most expatriates adapt to it easily and report that life in
Singapore is pleasant, relaxed and generally free of problems.

The EFL market is comparatively small, and conditions of work vary
considerably from employer to employer. Few schools recruit from
overseas, and even fewer will pay teachers' airfare or housing. However, working conditions are usually good, with most teachers having
to work only five days and 20-25 hours a week. Salaries are high and
teachers can save $600-$800 or more each month.

Berlitz Language Centre
501 Orchard Rd., B1-20, Orchard MRT Station, Singapore
238878
Tel: 733-7472

Brighton School
        51 Anson Road, Anson Centre, #05-53, Singapore 199748
        Tel: 221-7608   Fax: 221-7135
* The British Council (3 schools)
        30 Napier Road, Singapore 258509
        Tel: 473-1111   Fax: 472-1010
        E-mail: britcoun@britcoun.org.sg
ILC
        Cuppage Centre, 55 Cuppage Road, #08-21, Singapore
        229467
        Tel: 736-1707   Fax: 336-6554
inlingua School
        1 Grange Rd. 04-01 Orchard Building, Singapore 239693
        Tel: 737-6666   Fax: 467-5483
* International House (ATT)
        19 Tanglin Road # 08-01, Tanglin Shopping Centre,
        Singapore 247909
        Tel: 235-5222   Fax: 738-1257
        E-mail: attpr@singnet.com.sg
Language Systems Pte
        1 Sophia Road, Peace Centre, #07-01/04, Singapore
        228149
        Tel: 336-4222   Fax: 337-4854

South Korea   82

South Korea is one of the biggest TEFL markets in the world and it is open to both trained and untrained teachers. Unfortunately, it seems to produce more complaints from unhappy expatriate teachers than any other country in the world! This is partly because there are many unscrupulous employers among the owners of the hundreds of language schools ("hagwans") which opened in the past nine or ten years. However, it is also partly because Korea attracts many untrained teachers who travel there purely to make money. Most such teachers have no interest in learning about or adapting to a foreign culture, and they usually fail to do the research necessary for finding a suitable job. So, if you decide to go to Korea, you should be sure to research the job situation with great care.

Teachers who find jobs with reputable employers, including some of the universities, report that salaries and benefits packages are good, with most contracts providing airfare and accommodations. Teachers often work six days a week, teaching up to 35 hours, but they are able to save $500-$800 or even more a month. They also report that, while entertainment possibilities for expatriates tend to be very limited outside of Seoul, life in Korea can be both interesting and pleasant.

The Jobs Offered board at Dave's ESL Cafe (www.eslcafe.com) has a special section devoted to jobs in Korea. Anyone who is considering working in Korea should also make a point of reading the comments posted on the Job Discussion board at Dave's ESL Cafe. However, they should bear in mind that the postings often say more about the personality of the person who is posting than about the real situation of expatriate teachers in Korea.

Better Resource
> 3350 Wilshire Blvd., Suite 567, Los Angeles, CA 90010, USA
> Tel: (213) 738-1001   Fax: (213) 738-0852
> E-mail: better@wcis.com
> Website: www.eslkorea.com

* Andong National University Language Center
> Kyong-buk, Andong, Songchon-dong 388, 760-749 Republic of Korea
> Tel: (571) 50-5696   Fax: (571) 841-1629
> E-mail: afinch@anu.andong.ac.kr

Berlitz
> Sungwood Academy Building 2F, 1316-17 Seocho-Dong, Seochu-Gu, Seoul 137-074, Republic of Korea
> Tel: (2) 3481-5324   Fax: (2) 3481-3921
> E-mail: mpbubb@yahoo.com

Best Foreign Language Institute
> 98-3 Jungang-Dong, Changwon City, Kyungsangnam Province 641-030, Republic of Korea
> Tel: (551) 84-9544   Fax: (551) 83-08600

* David English House

    Namsandong 126-5, Kumjung-ku, Pusan 609-340, Republic of Korea

    Tel: (51) 516-7750   Fax: (51) 516-6307

Dong-A Foundation

    Daejeon Junior College, 226-2 Jayang-dong, Dong-ku, Daejeon 300-100, Republic of Korea

    Fax: (42) 625-5820

EEC International

    Fax: (2) 2225-5898

    E-mail: khchoe@eec.co.kr

ELSI / YBM (18 schools throughout Korea)

    649-1 Yeoksam-dong, Kangnam-gu, Seoul 135-081, Republic of Korea

    Tel: (2) 552-1492   Fax: (2) 501-2478

    E-mail: teach@ybmsisa.co.kr

    Website: www.ybmsisa.com

* International House Seoul

    Han Sung Technical College, 319-1 Hongje-dong, Seodaemoon-gu, Seoul, 120-090, Republic of Korea

    E-mail: kcnam@hansung.or.kr

    Website: www.hansung.or.kr

J.T. Language Institute

    618-1 Shinsadong, Kangnamgu, Seoul, Republic of Korea

    Fax: (2) 547-0647

Language Teaching Research Center

    60-17, 1-ka, Taepyong-Ro, Chung-gu, Seoul 100-101, Republic of Korea

    Tel: (2) 737-4641   Fax: (2) 734-6036

    E-mail: LTRC@unitel.co.kr

New Continental Foreign Language Institute (Suwon)

    Tel: (331) 222-5505   Fax: (331) 221-9971

    E-mail: ncfli@hotmail.com

Pagoda Language School

    56-6 2nd St., Jong-ro, Seoul 110-122, Republic of Korea

    Tel: (2) 267-2915   Fax: (2) 278-7538

SLS Language Institute
    45-1, Kongpyung-Dong, Joong-Gu, Taegu, Republic of
    Korea
    Tel: (53) 428-2992   Fax: (53) 431-0585
    E-mail: de_adams@hotmail.com
Sogang Language Programs Institute
    8th Floor, Young-Kwang Plazam 359-10, Jungga 1 Dong,
    Nowon Ku, Seoul, Republic of Korea
    Tel: (2) 952-8142   Fax: (2) 935-9821
    E-mail: tggodchild@hotmail.com
Sogang University
    English Language Dept., 1-1 Sinsu-dong, Mapo-gu, Seoul
    121-742, Republic of Korea
    Tel: (2) 716-1230   Fax: (2) 705-8733
    E-mail: jhong@ccs.sogang.ac.kr
Top Language School
    1266-14, 1-ka, Dukjin-dong, Dukjin-Ku, Jonju City,
    Jonbuk, Republic of Korea
    Tel: (652) 254-5090   Fax: (652) 74-4266
    E-mail: jade72@hotmail.com
Yes English School
    Daewon Building, 5th Floor, Daechi-dong 599, Kangnam-
    gu,Seoul 135-281, Republic of Korea
    Tel: (2) 553-8880   Fax: (2) 553-5764
    E-mail: yescho@nuri.net

Taiwan   **886**

Taiwan is a good TEFL market, but the earthquake of October 1999 has caused some disruption. However, given the resilience of the Taiwanese people, it is unlikely that this disruption will last long.

It is possible for both trained and untrained teachers to arrange jobs in advance from North America, but most employers prefer to hire teachers who are already in Taiwan. It should be noted that teachers who are hired from outside of Taiwan are normally provided with airfare and accommodations.

Salaries and working conditions are generally good, and teachers can often save $600-$1000 or more a month. However, they frequently teach six days and 30-35 hours a week.

Teachers report that Taiwan offers foreigners a comfortable lifestyle together with an opportunity to learn a lot about a fascinating and very different culture.

It should be noted that many (probably most) jobs involve teaching children, and that this is the cause of many complaints among foreign EFL teachers.

OEE Recruitment
    P O Box 274, Highland, WI 53543, USA
    Tel/Fax: (608) 929-4994
    E-mail: leyte@hotmail.com
Teachers in Asia
    630A Venice Blvd., Venice, CA 90291, USA
    Tel: (310) 574-7488   Fax: (310) 574-7489
    E-mail: danroth@loop.com
YMCA Overseas Service Corps
    101 North Wacker Drive, Chicago, IL 60606 IL, USA
    Tel: (800) 872-9622 ext. 343
    Fax: (312) 977-9036
Canadian-American Language Schools
    2 Jiau Hua Street, 2F, Hsinchu, Taiwan, ROC
    Fax: (3) 561-6905
    E-mail: employment@can-am.org
ELS International (16 schools throughout the country)
    12 Kuling Street, Taipei, Taiwan, ROC
    Tel: (2) 2321-9005   Fax: (2) 2397-2304
    E-mail: elsikk@tp.silkera.net
    Website: www.geocities.com/Athens/7304
David's English Center (Schools in several cities)
    3F, No. 100, Nanking E. Road, Taipei, Taiwan 104, ROC
    Tel: (2) 2522-4004   Fax: (2) 2521-9477
    E-mail: service@david.com.tw

Gram English Institute
    116 Yung Ho Road, 4th Fl. 116, Sec. 2, Yung Ho City,
    Taipei, Taiwan, ROC
    Tel: (2) 2927-2477   Fax: (2) 2926-2183
    E-mail: gram@ms7.hinet.net
    Website: www.gram.com.tw
Hess Educational Organization
    No. 419 Chung Shan Rd., Sec. 2, Chung Ho City 235,
    Taipei County, Taiwan, ROC
    Tel: (2) 3234-6188   Fax: (2) 3234-9488
    E-mail: hesswork@hess.com.tw
    Website: www.hess.com.tw
Jordan's Language School
    97 Chuan Chow Street, 1F, Taipei, Taiwan, ROC
    Tel: (2) 2332-5080   Fax: (2) 2305-1777
Language Training & Testing Center
    170 Hsin-hai Rd., Sec. 2, Taipei 106, Taiwan, ROC
    Tel: (2) 2362-6385   Fax: (2) 2367-1944
Line Up Language School
    398-1 Chihsien 1st Rd., @ Fl., Hsin-Hsing Area,
    Kaohsiung City, Taiwan, ROC
    Tel: (7) 235-8015   Fax: (7) 236-4311
    E-mail: DeeWinter@hotmail.com
Oxford Language & Computer Institute
    8 Fl., 240 Ching Shan 1st Rd., Kaohsiung, Taiwan, ROC
    Tel: (7) 281-2315   Fax: (7) 211-7119
* Shane English School
    5F, 41 Roosevelt Rd., Sec. 2, Taipei, Taiwan, ROC
    Tel: (2) 2351-7755   Fax: (2) 2397-2642
    E-mail: sest@ms12.hinet.net
Taipei Language Institute
    Kaohsiung Center 2F, 507 Chung Chan 2nd Road,
    Kaohsiung, Taiwan, ROC
    Tel: (7) 215-2965   Fax: (7) 215-2981

Thailand   **66**

Thailand has been a popular destination for foreign EFL teachers for over 30 years. They are attracted mainly by the fascinating local culture and ecology, and by the relaxed lifestyle which the country offers, at least to teachers outside of Bangkok. The latter city also attracts many foreigners, but most teachers appear to prefer the relative peace and tranquillity of smaller cities such as Chiang Mai.

The TEFL market continues to be generally healthy in spite of the economic recession of the late 1990's. It may be possible for trained teachers to arrange jobs from North America, but untrained teachers almost always have to travel to Thailand to find work. Employers rarely pay airfare or accommodation costs. (Luckily, accommodations are comparatively inexpensive and easy to find, and so this is not a major problem.)

Unlike in many other Asian countries, teachers usually teach only five days and 20-25 hours a week. Inevitably, this means that salaries are much lower than in countries such as Japan or Korea. However, teachers frequently choose to teach overtime or private lessons to increase their earnings. Most teachers report that they can save $400-$500 a month without too much difficulty and while still being able to enjoy a comfortable lifestyle.

AUA Language Center
    179 Rajadamri Rd., Bangkok 10330, Thailand
    Tel: (2) 252-8170   Fax: (2) 255-4632
AUA Language Center
    73 Rajadamnern Rd., Amphur Muang, Chiang Mai 50200,
    Thailand
    Tel/Fax: (53) 211-973
* Chiang Mai University
    Dept. of English, 239 Huay Kaew Rd., Amphur Muang,
    Chiang Mai 50200, Thailand
    Tel/Fax: (53) 943-258
ECC
    430 / 17-24 Chula Soi 64, Siam Sq., Bangkok 10330,
    Thailand

Tel: (2) 253-3312   Fax: (2) 254-2243
E-mail: eccthai@comnet3.ksc.net.th
Website: www.u-net.com/eflweb/schools/ECC/index.htm
Elite Training Institute
2nd Floor, Kongboonma Building, 699 Silom Rd., 10500
Bangkok, Thailand
Tel: (2) 233-6620
E-mail: elite_training@hotmail.com
ELS International   (7 schools in Thailand)
419 / 3 Rajavithee Rd., Phyathai (Opposite Children's
Hospital), Bangkok 10400, Thailand
Tel: (2) 247-8088   Fax: (2) 246-4365
E-mail: elsthai@ksc.th.com
Inlingua School
7th Floor, Central Chidlom Tower, 22 Ploenchit Rd.,
Pathumwan, Bangkok 10330, Thailand
Tel: (2) 254-7029   Fax: (2) 254-7098
E-mail: executrn@ksc5.th.com
Fun Language International
275 Lee House, 4 / F, Thonglor Soi 13, Sukhumvit 55,
Bangkok, Thailand
Fax: (2) 712-7733
E-mail: engisfun@loxinfo.co.th
King's College of English
Central City Office Tower, Floor 5A, Central City Bangna,
Bangna-Trad Rd., Prakanang, Bangkok, Thailand
Tel: (2) 745-6001   Fax: (2) 745-6000
E-mail: kingth@asiaaccess.net.th
* North American Language School
36 / 1 Ngam Wongwam Rd., Bangkok 10900, Thailand
Tel: (2) 953-0416   Fax: (2) 953-0417
E-mail: northam2000@yahoo.com
Siam Computer & Language Institute
471 / 19 Ratchawithi Rd., Bangkok 10400, Thailand
Tel: (2) 247-2345   Fax: (2) 644-6974

Siam Computer & Language School
    2 Soi, 7 Phung-nga Rd., Muang, Phuket 83000, Thailand
    Tel: (76) 219-914   Fax: (76) 218-720
    E-mail: narisara@phuket.a-net.net.th

Stamford College
    Soi Ju-teeuthit 3, HatYai, Songkhia 90110, Thailand
    Tel: (74) 347-203   Fax: (74) 347-201
    E-mail: chain@hatyai.inet.co.th

TCD Co. Ltd.
    399 / 7 Soi Thongloh 21, Sukhumvit Soi 55, Bangkok
    10110, Thailand
    Tel: (2) 712-8503   Fax: (2) 391-5670

Vietnam   84

Vietnam is a comparatively new TEFL market but it is expanding rapidly and offers many opportunities for foreign teachers. Facilities and amenities are still comparatively poor, and there is little accessible entertainment for foreigners. In spite of this, North Americans working there have a fairly comfortable life and seem to enjoy the country, the people and the teaching. They are particularly impressed by the warm welcome which they receive from most local people.

Most jobs are arranged on the spot rather than from outside of Vietnam, and few employers pay airfare or accommodation. Teachers normally work five days and 20-25 hours a week, for a base salary which allows a reasonable lifestyle. However, they report that there are many opportunities for teaching extra private lessons, which can enable teachers to save $500 or more each month.

Almost all jobs which are advertised are located in Hanoi or Ho Chi Minh City, with the latter having the giant's share of the market. Job possibilities in other towns would have to be researched locally.

World University Service of Canada
    Recruitment Section, P O Box 3000, Station C, Ottawa,
    Ontario, K1Y 4M8 Canada
    Fax: (613) 798-0990
    E-mail: recruit@wusc.ca

American Language Institute
> 87C Tho Nhuom Street, Hanoi, Vietnam
> Tel: (4) 934-0263

* Apollo Education Centre
> 191 Tay Son, Dong Da, Hanoi, Vietnam
> Tel: (4) 857-0620   Fax: (4) 857-0637
> E-mail: Apollo@netnam.org.vn

BEST Services
> 81A Nguyen Son Ha St., Ward 5, District 3, Ho Chi Minh
> City, Vietnam
> Tel: (8) 830-0363   Fax: (8) 830-0364
> E-mail: best-hq@bdvn.vnd.net

* The British Council
> 1813 Cao Ba Quat, Ba Dinh District, Hanoi, Vietnam
> Tel: (4) 843-4941   Fax: (4) 843-4962
> E-mail: bchanoi@netnam.org.m

Centre for Foreign Languages
> College of Agriculture & Forestry, Vietnam National
> University, Ap an Nhon, Xa Tan Phu, Thu Duc District, Ho
> Chi Minh City, Vietnam
> Tel: (8) 896-0109   Fax: (8) 896-3349
> E-mail: dhthinh@hcm.vnn.vn

Danang Foreign Languages Teachers' College
> 17 Le Duan Street, Danang, Vietnam
> Fax: (84) 512-3683

ELT Lotus
> 53 Nguyen Du St., District 1, Ho Chi Minh City, Vietnam
> Tel: (8) 251-556   Fax: (8) 330-059

* International House Hanoi
> 67 Le Van Huu St., Hanoi, Vietnam
> E-mail: hanoi@apolloedutrain.com
> Website: www.apolloedutrain.com

* International House Ho Chi Minh City
> 3rd Floor, 146 AB Pasteur St., District 1,
> Ho Chi Minh City, Vietnam
> E-mail: hcmc@apolooedutrain.com

Language Link

    64 Nguyen Truong Street, Hanoi, Vietnam

    Tel: (4) 829-4844

Minh Hoa Tescan

    20/B-60, 3 Yhang 2 Street, Ward 12, District 10, Ho Chi Minh City, Vietnam

    Tel/Fax: (8) 654-977

School of Languages & Information Technology

    45 Ngo Duc Ke, D1, Ho Chi Minh City, Vietnam

    Tel: (8) 290-644   Fax: (8) 294-092

Vietnam America Society

    109 Pasteur Street, District 3, Ho Chi Minh City, Vietnam

    Tel: (8) 829-4834   Fax: (8) 823-6002

    E-mail: ctavhm@netnam2.org.vn

EUROPE (EU COUNTRIES)

Western Europe is undoubtedly one of the most attractive areas for North Americans looking to live and work overseas. Unfortunately, most Western European countries are now part of the European Union, which makes it almost impossible for citizens of non-EU countries to arrange legal work in the member countries.

In theory, non-EU citizens can still apply for TEFL jobs in Western Europe. Once they have obtained a job offer, they or their employer can apply for the necessary work permit and residence visa. However, in practice, few employers are willing to undertake the expense and the bureaucratic work which is involved in this process, particularly since they can employ British or Irish teachers with virtually no effort.

In some countries, most notably Germany, it is sometimes possible for foreign teachers to obtain legal status by registering as free-lance or independent workers. Unfortunately, the regulations which govern this process tend to change frequently and to be applied in a haphazard manner from country to country (and even from one local office to another).

In spite of these complications, many Americans and Canadians still manage to teach EFL in EU countries either by obtaining EU citizenship or by working illegally.

Obtaining EU Citizenship

Some North Americans are able to obtain citizenship of an EU country by virtue of having a parent or grandparent who emigrated to Canada or the USA from that country. The regulations and the bureaucratic process involved vary considerably from country to country. In Italy for example, citizenship is granted only to people with a parent who was born in Italy. In the case of Ireland, however, citizenship is granted to people who have an Irish parent or grandparent.

If you have parents or grandparents from an EU country and you are interested in the possibility of obtaining citizenship, you should get in touch with the nearest consulate of the country concerned. They will be able to tell you whether you are eligible for citizenship and, if so, how the application process operates.

It is also possible to obtain EU work and residence rights by marrying a citizen of an EU country.

Working Illegally

Most of the thousands of Canadians and Americans who teach EFL in EU countries do so illegally. They travel to a European country as tourists and then find illegal jobs with employers who pay them in cash. When their tourist visas expire, they leave the country for a weekend and then reenter as tourists. Some people manage to do this for years, particularly in Mediterranean countries such as Greece, where immigration and work regulations are less rigorously enforced.

You should note that people who teach illegally within the EU have no employment protection. They are also subject to legal penalties, including deportation.

How To Find Work

There is no magic formula for finding a TEFL position in Europe. However, if you are determined to look for work in one of the EU countries, the following pieces of advice may help you to approach your job search in the most productive manner:

- Take a TEFL training /certification course before you go. This is really the best way to maximize your chances of finding a TEFL job in Europe. If at all possible, take an RSA/Cambridge CELTA (or, failing this, a Trinity College TESOL Certificate) course, since many European employers do not recognize other types of TEFL certification.

- It is rarely worthwhile contacting schools before you arrive in Europe. Whether you have an EU passport or not, the only way you will be able to find work in EU countries is by going there and contacting employers on the spot. However many letters you write in advance, you will almost certainly not receive a job offer.

- Aim to arrive in September or October, as that is when more than 80% of jobs start. Failing that, the next best time to arrive is in early January. (In the case of Greece, the very best time to arrive is in early January.)

- Bring with you a return air ticket, plus enough money to allow you to live for at least eight weeks.

- When you arrive in your target city, get an up-to-date list of the country's language schools from the local offices of the British Council. Supplement this list with addresses of schools from the local telephone yellow pages.

- Visit every language school that you can find and leave a copy of your resume. If you can, talk with the school's director of studies to find out whether there is any real possibility of your getting a job with the school.

- If you have not received any positive or encouraging reactions after contacting all of the schools, accept that you have exhausted the local job possibilities. Then decide if you should return home or move to another city (or country) and try again!

The following list includes British Council branches, together with other offices which issue lists of language schools. Some of the offices will agree to mail you the lists but others will insist that you visit them in person to obtain the lists.

English International produces a PC disk which contains the most comprehensive list of EFL schools currently available anywhere. Details of the disk, which includes the addresses of 500 EU schools, can be found at the E.I. website (www.english-international.com).

Austria   43

The British Council
      Schenkenstrasse 4, A-1010 Vienna, Austria
      Tel: (1) 533 26 16 82   Fax: (1) 533 26 16 85
      E-mail: information@bc-vienna.at
Verband Osterreichischer Volkshochschulen
      Weintraubengasse 13, 1020 Vienna, Austria

Belgium   **32**

The British Council
    Liefdadighheidstraat 15, 1210 Brussels, Belgium
    Tel: (2) 227 08 40   Fax: ((2) 227 08 49

Denmark   **45**

The British Council
    Gammel Mont 12, 1117 Copenhagen K, Denmark
    Tel: (33) 36 94 00   Fax: (33) 36 94 06

France   **33**

The British Council
    9-11 rue de Constantine, 75340 Paris, France
    Tel: (1) 55 73 23   Fax: (1) 55 73 02
    E-mail: library@bc-paris.bcouncil.org

Finland   **358**

The British Council
    Hakaniemenkatu 2, 00530 Helsinki, Finland
    Tel: (9) 701 8731
FFBS
    Puistokatu 1 b A, 00140 Helsinki, Finland
    Tel/Fax: (9) 629 626

Germany   **49**

The British Council
    Hardenbergstr. 20, 10623 Berlin, Germany
    Tel: (30) 311 0990   Fax: (30) 311 0992
    E-mail: bc.berlin@britcoun.de
The British Council
    Katherinenstr. 1-3, 04109 Leipzig, Germany
    Tel: (341) 140 641 11   Fax: (341) 140 641 41
    E-mail: Bettina.Kreuzburg@britcoun.de

The British Council
Rumfordstr. 7, 80469 Munich, Germany
Tel: (89) 29 00 86 0   Fax: (89) 29 00 86 88
E-mail: bc.munich@britcoun.de

Greece   30

The British Council
14 Lykavitou Street, Kolonaki, Athens, Greece
Tel: (1) 369 2333   Fax: (1) 363 0481
E-mail: eduinfo@britcoun.gr
PALSO
2 Lykavitou St., 106 71 Kolonaki, Athens, Greece
Tel: (1) 364 0792   Fax: (1) 364 2359

Italy   39

AISLI
Via Campanella 16, 41100 Modena, Italy
E-mail: timp@teleion.it
The British Council
Via Quattro Fontane 20, 00184 Rome, Italy
Tel: (6) 478 141   Fax: (6) 481 4296
E-mail: Info.Rome@BritCoun.it

Netherlands   31

The British Council
Keizersgracht 269, 1016 ED Amsterdam, Netherlands
Tel: (20) 550 6060   Fax: (20) 602 7389
E-mail: education.info@britcoun.nl

Portugal   351

The British Council
Rua de Sao Marcal 174, 1249-062 Lisbon, Portugal
Tel: (1) 347 6141   Fax: (1) 347 6151
E-mail: fred.ohalon@britcounpt.org

Spain   34

ACADE

Avda. Alberto Alcocer 46, 28016 Madrid, Spain
Tel: (1) 344 0915   Fax: (1) 344 1583
The British Council
Paseo del General Martinez Campos 31, 28010 Madrid, Spain
Tel: (1) 337 3551   Fax: (1) 337 3570
E-mail: information@es-britcoun.org
The British Council
Calle Amigo 83, 08021 Barcelona, Spain
Tel: (3) 209 1364

Sweden   46

The British Council
c/o The British Embassy, P O Box 27819, S-115 93 Stockholm, Sweden
Tel: (8) 663 6004   Fax: (8) 663 7271
Folkuniversity
Rehnsgatan 20, Box 7845, 10398 Stockholm, Sweden
Tel: (8) 789 4100   Fax: (8) 166 478

EUROPE (Non-EU Countries)

Most TEFL jobs in the non-EU countries of Europe are in private language schools located in the former Eastern Bloc countries. Job opportunities are particularly good in Hungary, Poland and the Czech Republic. There are limited opportunities for foreign (including North American) teachers in many of the other countries in the region, although rarely in either Norway or Switzerland.

The better jobs tend to be with schools which are owned by or are affiliated with British-based TEFL organizations such as International House, EF and Language Link. As a general rule, these schools will hire only teachers who have a TEFL certificate, preferably the RSA/ Cambridge CELTA or the Trinity College TESOL Certificate.

Trained teachers can usually arrange jobs in advance, whereas other teachers will normally have to travel to the country to arrange work. Employers rarely if ever pay airfare but some schools will provide free housing.

Housing in the former Eastern Bloc countries is often cramped and primitive by North American standards, and even teachers who live in major cities are frequently surprised by the lack of basic amenities, facilities and resources. However, foreigners find it relatively easy to mix with local people and they usually have access (at least in the big cities and university towns) to quite a wide range of entertainments and cultural activities.

Most jobs require teachers to work only five days and 18-24 hours a week. Salaries are generally adequate to permit a comfortable (in local terms) lifestyle, as well as limited travel within the country and the surrounding region. Savings are rarely possible, and teachers in poorer countries such as Bulgaria and Albania sometimes have to subsidize their time overseas.

The best countries for new teachers to try are probably Poland and the Czech Republic, since these have the biggest TEFL markets. They also usually permit a more comfortable lifestyle than many of the other countries.

Armenia

* International House Yerevan
  Apt. 13, Abovyan St. 41, Str. H. Hakdoyan 1,
  Yerevan 375033, 375009 Armenia
  E-mail: softsafe@hotmail.com
  Website: www.softsafe.am

Azerbaijan

* International House Baku
  Khagani 20/20, Baku, 37001 Azerbaijan
  E-mail: intellect@azerin.com

Belarus   375

* International House
  Room 306, Gykalo 9, Minsk 220071, Belarus
  Tel: (172) 32 47 12   Fax: (172) 31 60 07
  E-mail: ih@user.unibel.by   Website: www.ih.unibel.by

Bulgaria   359

Private School For Banking & Business
  83 Bogomil Street, Plovdiv, Bulgaria
  Tel: (32) 68 14 14   Fax: (32) 27 48 80

Croatia   385

Lancon English Language Consultancy
  Kumiciceva 10, 10 000 Zagreb, Croatia
  Tel: (1) 455-2631   Fax: (1) 455-5697
  E-mail: lmo@lancon.hr
  Website: www. Lancon.hr/lancon
Vern Lingua
  Senoina 28, 10 000 Zagreb, Croatia
  Tel: (1) 428-548

Cyprus   357

The British Council
   3 Museum St., P O Box 5654, Nicosia, Cyprus
   Tel: (2) 44 21 52

Czech Republic   420

The capital city, Prague, currently has more than a hundred language schools, some of which employ scores of foreign teachers. However, many teachers living in Prague complain that the city is comparatively expensive and that accommodations are generally poor and overpriced. So it is better for new teachers to look for work in other cities, such as Pilsen or Brno, both of which have thriving TEFL markets.

Academic Information Agency (Public schools)
   Dumzahranicnich sluzeb MSMT, Senovazne nam. 26, 111
   21 Prague 1, Czech Republic
   Tel: (2) 24 22 96 98
   E-mail: aia@dzs.cz
   Website: www.dzs.cz
* Caledonian School (Schools in Prague and Bratislava)
   Vitavska 24, 150 00 Prague 5, Czech Republic
   Tel: (2) 57 31 36 50
   E-mail: jobs@caledonianschool.com
   Website: caledonianschool.com
* ILC International House
   Sokolska 1, 602 00 Brno, Czech Republic
   Tel: (5) 41 24 04 93   Fax: (5) 41 24 59 54
   E-mail: ihbrno@sky.cz
   Website: www.ilcgroup.com
* ILC International House
   Lupacova 1, 130 00 Prague, Czech Republic
   Tel: (2) 697 45 13   Fax: (2) 231 85 84
   E-mail: ihprague@telecom.cz
   Website: www.ilcgroup.com

* Elvis Jazykova Skola
    Dacickeho 8, 140 00 Prague 4, Czech Republic
    Tel: (2) 42 00 44
    E-mail: info@elvis.cz
Prague Language Centre
    V Jame 8, 110 00 Prague 1, Czech Republic
    Tel: (2) 26 23 55
    E-mail: plc@mbox.vol.cz
Cosmolingua
    Zdarila 8, 140 00 Prague 4, Czech Republic
    Tel: (2) 61 22 56 90
    E-mail: praha@cosmolingua.cz

Estonia   372

* International House
    Pikk 69, Tallinn EE 0001, Estonia
    Tel: 641-0607   Fax: 641-1407
    E-mail: ihte@online.ee
* International Language Services
    Pikk 9m, Tallinn EE001, Estonia
    Tel: 646-4258   Fax: 641-2475
    E-mail: ilsinfo@online.ee
    Website: www.online.ee/~ilsinfo

Hungary   36

Hungary is a very sophisticated country with a good TEFL market. Foreign teachers can find jobs which provide good facilities and working conditions, and which permit a comfortable lifestyle. Those who work in Budapest will also have access to a wide range of entertainments.

The job market is highly competitive, particularly in Budapest, and most schools hire only teachers with a TEFL certificate and/or previous experience. Except in smaller towns, the only TEFL certificates which are normally recognized are the Cambridge CELTA and the Trinity College TESOL Certificate.

SPUSA Education Center
    Navratilova 2, 110 00 Prague 1, Czech Republic
    Tel: (2) 22 23 17 02   Fax: (2) 22 23 25 30
Languages At Work
    Na Florenci 35, 110 00 Prague 1, Czech Republic
    Tel: (2) 24 81 13 79
    E-mail: employment@mbox.vol.cz
    Website: www.vol.cz/atwork
* Akcent Language School
    Bitovska 3, 140 00 Prague 4, Czech Republic
    Tel: (2) 42 05 95   Fax: (2) 42 28 45
    E-mail: info.akcent@akcent.cz
Atalanta Business & Language School
    Visregradi u. 9, 1132 Budapest, Hungary
    Tel: (1) 131-4954
    E-mail: atalanta.marketing@atalanta.datanet.hu
IHH A Nyelviskola
    Teleki u. 18, 9022 Gyor, Hungary
    Tel: (96) 315-444   Fax: (96) 315-665
* International House
    P O Box 95, Budapest 1364, Hungary
    Tel: (1) 212-4010   Fax: (1) 316-2491
    E-mail: bp@ih.hu
    Website: www.ih.hu
* International House
    Mecset utca. 3, Eger 3300, Hungary
    Tel: (36) 413- 770
    E-mail: iheger@mail.matav.hu
* Bell Iskolak
    Tulipan u. 8, 1022 Budapest, Hungary
    Tel: (1) 212-4324   Fax: (1) 326-5033
    E-mail: bellisk@mail.matav.hu
Vaci Street Development Centre
    Terez Krt. 47, 1067 Budapest, Hungary
    Tel: (1) 302-2214   Fax: (1) 353-3274
    E-mail: bruce@mail.inext.hu

* EF English First
  Kosciuskos g. 11, 2000 Vilnius, Lithuania
  Tel: (2) 791-616   Fax: (2) 791-646
Dept. of Foreign Relations
  Ministry of Education and Science, Volano Gatve 2/7,
  2691 Vilnius, Lithuania
  Tel: (2) 622-483   Fax: (2) 612-077
* Soros International House
  Gedimino 47, 3000 Kaunas, Lithuania
  Tel/Fax: (7) 22 4-166
  E-mail: rita@ih.kau.osf.lt
* Soros International House
  Ukmerges 41, 2662 Vilnius, Lithuania
  Tel: (2) 724-879   Fax: (2) 724- 839
  E-mail: daiva@ihouse.osf.lt
  Website: www.nkm.lt/724839.html
Klaipeda International School of Languages
  Zveju 2, Klaipeda 5800, Lithuania
  Tel: (6) 311-1190
  E-mail: mark.uribe@klaipeda.omnitel.net

Macedonia   389

* Soros International House - Habil Oy
  Nikola Parapunov b.b., 91000 Skopje, Macedonia
  Tel: (91) 364-625   Fax: (91) 364-596
  E-mail: keitha@bogomil.soros.org.mk
* St George's School of English
  Partizanski odredi 3-3/5, 91000 Skopje, Macedonia
  Tel: (91)125-280   E-mail: stevedan@mol.com.mk

Malta   356

Malta is a beautiful country with a small but thriving TEFL market.
Unfortunately, it is virtually impossible for foreign teachers to obtain
work permits and jobs.

Latvia 371

English Language Centre Satva
Office 8, 79/85 Dzirnavu Str., 1011 Riga, Latvia
Tel: 722-6641

Lithuania 370

American Partnership for Lithuanian Education
P O Box 617, Durham, CT 06422, USA
Tel: (203) 347-7095   Fax: (203) 327-5837
Educational English Culture
Villa Monaco, Sliema Rd., Kappara SGN 06, Malta
Tel: 313-033   Fax: 314-523
Inlingua
9 Triq Guze Fava, Tower Rd., Sliema SLM 15, Malta
Tel: 336-384   Fax: 336-419

Norway 47

The British Council
Fridtjof Nansens Plass 5, 0188 Oslo, Norway
E-mail: british.council@britcoun.no

Poland 48

Poland currently has perhaps the largest TEFL market in Europe, and there are almost limitless opportunities for both trained and untrained teachers from North America. Trained teachers should be able to arrange a job in advance from North America, but teachers without TEFL training will almost certainly have to travel to Poland to find work. Some of the best jobs are with International House schools; however, these schools normally employ only teachers with the CELTA.

A large number of jobs are available in the capital, Warsaw, but many teachers prefer to work in smaller, more attractive cities such as Poznan and Krakow, where teachers generally enjoy a more relaxed lifestyle and where housing is less expensive.

AAE (American Academy of English) USA
   2110 N. Military Road, Arlington, VA 22207, USA
   Fax: (703) 448-9498   E-mail: info@ameracad.com
   Website: www.ameracad.com
American Academy of English
   ul. Slowackiego 16, Katowice 40-094, Poland
   Tel: (32) 253-0272   E-mail: aae@silesia.top.pl
   Website: aae@silter.silesia.top.pl
Angloschool (5 schools in Warsaw)
   ul. Ks. J. Popieuszki 7, 01-786 Warsaw, Poland
   Tel: 663-8883   Fax: 639-8124
   E-mail: angloschool@angloschool.com.pl
* BEST
   ul. Pestazziego 11/13, 80-445 Gdansk, Poland
   Tel: (58) 344-3474   E-mail: bestudu@ikp.atm.com.pl
* EF English First (Schools in Warsaw, Lodz and Bydgoszcz)
   Smolna 8 p XVIII, 00-375 Warsaw, Poland
   Tel: (22) 826-0871   Fax: (22) 826-8206
   E-mail: ef-1@ef.com.pl
English School of Communication Skills
   ul. Bernardynska 15, 13-100 Tarnow, Poland
   Tel: (14) 213-769   E-mail: personnel@escs.pl
* International House
   ul. Krasinskiego 24, 43-300 Bielsko Biala, Poland
   Tel: (33) 811-7927   Fax: (33) 811-0229
   E-mail: ihbb@silesia.top.pl
   Website: www.silesia.top.pl/~ihih/bielsko
* International House
   ul. Dworcowa 81, 85-009 Bydgoszcz, Poland
   Tel: (52) 22-35-15   Tel/Fax: (52) 22-34-44
   E-mail: inthouse@cps.pl
* International House
   ul. Sokolska 78/80, 40-1287 Katowice, Poland
   Tel/Fax: (32) 253-8833
   E-mail: ihih@silesia.top.pl
   Website: www.silesia.top.pl/~ihih/katowice

* International House
ul. Targowa 18, 1p, 108, 25-520 Kielce, Poland
Tel: (41) 343-0258   Fax: (41) 343-0261
E-mail: kielce@ih.pl   Website: www.ih.pl
* International House
ul. Zwyciestwa 7/9, 75-028 Koszalin, Poland
Tel: (94) 41-01-96   Fax: (94) 41-01-80
* International House
ul. Pilsudskiego 6, 31-109 Krakow, Poland
Tel: (12) 421-9440   Fax: (12) 421-8652
E-mail: admin@ih.pl
Website: www.ih.pl
* International House
ul. Zielona 15, 90-601 Lodz, Poland
Tel: (42) 300-0 26   Fax: (42) 300-028
E-mail: lodz@ih.pl
Website: www.ih.pl
* International House
ul. Kosciuszki 17, 45-062 Opole, Poland
Tel: (77) 56-5695   Fax: (77) 54-6655
E-mail: ihih@silesia.top.pl
Website: www.silesia.top.pl/~ihih/opole
* International House
ul. Sw. Marcin 66/72, 61-807 Poznan, Poland
Tel: (61) 851-6453   Fax: (61) 851-6171
* International House
ul. Legionow 15, 87-100 Torun, Poland
Tel: (56) 25-081   Fax: (56) 622-5081
E-mail: ihtorun@ikp.atm.com.pl
* International House
ul. Ruska 46a, 50-079 Wroclaw, Poland
Tel: (71) 372-3698   E-mail: wrocdos@id.pl
Website: www.silesia.top.pl/~ihih/wroclaw
JDJ Service
ul. Gronowa 22, pol.615-621 Vlp, 61-655 Poznan, Poland
Tel: (61) 820-3159   E-mail: jdj-hq@ikp.atm.com.pl

Lang LTC
    ul. Niepodleglosci 217 m. 8, 02-087 Warsaw, Poland
    Tel: (22) 825-3940   Fax: (22) 825-2273
    E-mail: clientserv@lang.com.pl
Lektor Szkola Jezydow Obcych
    ul. Olawska 2, 50-123, Wroclaw, Poland
    Tel: (71) 343-2599
Stairway School of English
    ul. Dunajewskiego 6/415, 31-133 Krakow, Poland
    Tel: (12) 244-1836
* Target Professional English
    ul. Polna 50 7p, 00-644 Warsaw, Poland
    Tel: (22) 660-7029   E-mail: targeted@it.com.pl

Romania   40

* International House Language Centre
    Bd. Republicii 9, 1900 Timisoara, Romania
    Tel/Fax: (56) 190-593
    E-mail: rodica@ihlctim.sorostm.ro
    Website: www.sorostm.ro/ih/
Open Doors School of English
    Str. L Blaga 4, 1900 Timisoara, Romania
    Tel: (56) 302-201   Fax: (56) 194-252
    E-mail: michelle@online.ro

Russia   7

The economic and social situation remains unsettled throughout Russia and life for foreigners can be very challenging, particularly in Moscow. However, the TEFL job market continues to be fairly strong, notably in St. Petersburg and in/around Moscow.

Teachers with a recognized TEFL certificate, such as the CELTA, should have no problem arranging jobs in advance with such large and reputable school groups as International House, EF and Language Link. Other teachers should note that conditions of work vary greatly from school to school, and they should take care to research prospective employers with care.

Benedict Schools
   23 ul. Pskovskaya, St. Petersburg 190008, Russia
   Tel: (812) 113-8568   Fax: (812) 114-4445
   E-mail: benedict@infopro.spb.su
* BKC - International House (Moscow and St. Petersburg)
   Tverskaya ul., Dom 9A, Bld 4, 103009 Moscow, Russia
   Tel: (095) 234-0314   Fax: (095) 234-0316
   E-mail: info@bkc.ru
   Website: www.bkc.ru
* Centre for Education 'Grint' (Moscow)
   Tel: (095) 374-7430   Fax: (095) 374-7366
   E-mail: info@grint.ru
   Website: www.grint.ru
* EF English First
   125 Brestskaya 1st Street, 5th Fl, 125047 Moscow,
   Russia
   Tel: (095) 937-3886   Fax: (095) 937-3889
English School Sunny Plus
   P O Box 23, 125057 Moscow, Russia
   Tel: (095) 151-2500
   E-mail: sunnyplus@glasnet.ru
   Website: www.sunnyplus.ru
* Language Link Schools
   Novoslobodskaya ul, 5, bld. 2, 103030 Moscow, Russia
   Tel: (095) 234-0703
   E-mail: jobs@language.ru
   Website: www.language.ru
Polyglot International Language Academy
   Block 5, 19 Novyasenevsky Prospect, Moscow 117593,
   Russia
   Tel: (095) 281-2860
   E-mail: polyglot@glasnet.ru

Slovakia   421

City University Slovakia
    Human Resources Dept., City University, 335 116th
    Avenue SE, Bellevue, WA 98004, USA
    Tel: (425) 637-1010   Fax: (425) 637-9689
    E-mail: sanderson@cityu.edu
Akademia Vzdelavania
    Gorkeho 10, 815 17 Bratislava, Slovak Republic
    Tel: (7) 531- 0042   Fax: (7) 531- 0040
    E-mail: hviscova@aveducation.sk
Flosculus
    Drevny trh. 5, 040 01 Kosice, Slovak Republic
    Tel: (95) 622-5149
    E-mail: flos@ke.pubnet.sk

Slovenia   386

* Nista Language School
    Kidriceva 44, 6000 Koper, Sloenia
    Tel: (66) 271-271
Jezikovni Center International
    Gornji Trg 4, 1101 Ljubljana
    Tel: (61) 125-5317   Fax: (61) 226-167

Switzerland   41

Switzerland is one of the most affluent countries in the world, and it
has an excellent TEFL market. Unfortunately, the government is very
reluctant to allow foreign teachers to work in the country and so job
prospects for North Americans are extremely limited.

Any Swiss consulate can provide a handbook listing language schools
and other potential employers throughout the country. You should
also be able to obtain a list of possible employers from:

Service Scolaire, 16 rue du Mont Blanc, P O Box 1488, 1211 Geneva
1, Switzerland.

Berlitz

    1 Carrefour de Rive, CH-1207 Geneva, Switzerland
    Tel: (22) 718 38 90   Fax: (22) 718 38 91
    E-mail: geneve1@berlitz.ch

Berlitz

    Seefeldstrasse 7, CH-8008 Zurich, Switzerland
    Tel: (1) 256 88 70   Fax: (1) 256 88 71

inlingua

    Dufourstrasse 50, CH-4052 Basel, Switzerland
    Tel: (61) 278 99 33   Fax: (61) 278 99 30
    E-mail: Sprachkurse@inlingua-basel.ch

inlingua

    Rue du Leman 6, CH-1201 Geneva, Switzerland
    Tel: (22) 732 40 20   Fax: (22) 731 42 66

inlingua

    Grand Pont 18, CH-1003 Lausanne, Switzerland
    Tel: (21) 323 94 15   Fax: (21) 323 26 79

Wall Street Institute

    Effingerstrasse 53, 3008 Bern, Switzerland
    Tel: (31) 382 22 29   Fax: (31) 382 44 01

Wall Street Institute

    Rue de Lausanne, 18-20 Centre Commercial "Les Cygnes,"
    1201 Geneva, Switzerland
    Tel: (22) 738 11 41   Fax: (22) 738 20 79

Wall Street Institute

    Rue du Simplon 34, 1006 Lausanne, Switzerland
    Tel: (21) 614 66 01   Fax: (21) 614 66 65

Ukraine   **380**

* International House

    7 Marshala Bazhanova Street, 310002 Kharkiv, Ukraine
    Tel: (572) 400-417   Fax: (572) 141-109
    E-mail: ih@i-house.kharkov.ua

* International House

    7 V. Vasilevskoy Street, 252055 Kiyv, p/b 6411 Kiyv,

Ukraine
Tel: (44) 271-0870   Tel/Fax: (44) 274-2264
E-mail: school@sihs.kiev.ua
* International House
    109 Zelena Street, Lviv 290035, Ukraine
    Tel/Fax: (322) 72-60-68
    E-mail: marianna@sihs.lviv.ua
* International House
    27a pr. Shevchenko, Odessa 270058, Ukraine
    Tel: (482) 42-97-02   Fax: (482) 42-97-03
    E-mail: tsinipol@te.net.ua
* London School of English
    Central Post Office, Box 'B' 158, 242001 Kiev, Ukraine
    Tel: (44) 241-8654
    E-mail: admin@lse.kiev.ua
Monarch International Language Academy
    8 Vorovskogo Street, 252000 Kiev, Ukraine
    Tel: (44) 212-0206   Fax: (44) 212-5683

Yugoslavia   381

Galindo Skola (Sava Centar)
    Milentija Popovica 9, 11070 Novi Boegrad, Yugoslavia
    Tel: (11) 311-4568   Fax: (11) 455-785
    E-mail: galindo@net.yu

LATIN AMERICA

Latin America is a huge TEFL market but jobs vary greatly in quality from country to country, and even within individual countries. So it is important that prospective teachers make every effort to research the market carefully and to check out employers and agents who offer TEFL jobs.

Many positions are open to unqualified teachers, but most of the better employers now recruit only teachers who have a BA/BS degree and/or a TEFL certificate.

Some jobs can be arranged in advance, by responding to ads or by contacting schools direct. However, many employers offer contracts only to applicants who are willing to travel to the country for interview. This is particularly likely to be the case with untrained teachers or with teachers who have never lived overseas.

Mexico is the easiest country in which to find a job, even for teachers who have no formal qualifications or training. It is probably also the easiest country for Americans and Canadians to adapt to.

Central America is another area where work is easy to find, but most jobs in that region offer poor working conditions and only survival salaries. Further south, the largest TEFL markets are in Brazil and Argentina, followed by Colombia and Ecuador; all of these countries offer comparatively good working conditions. A very much smaller number of jobs are available in Venezuela, Peru, Chile, Bolivia and Uruguay.

Prearranged contracts are usually for one year, renewable by mutual consent. Work which is arranged locally may be on a more flexible, month-by-month basis. In most areas, work is available at any time of the year, although few jobs in South American begin between November and February.

Most jobs require teachers to work 18-24 hours per week, Monday through Friday, and year contracts usually include 4-6 weeks of paid vacation. Even in the richer countries, salaries are rarely high enough to permit savings of more than $200-$300 a month, unless teachers supplement them with income from overtime or private lessons. Very few employers in Latin America pay airfares for new teachers. Although schools will frequently help new arrivals to find suitable accommodations, they do not normally pay the cost of housing.

Argentina   54

** ALICANA
   San Martin 2293, 3000 Santa Fe, Argentina
   Tel: (42) 53-7567   Fax: (42) 55-2026
** AMICANA
   Chile 985, 5500 Mendoza, Argentina
   Tel: (61) 23-6271   Fax: (61) 29-8702
   E-mail: amicana@impsat.com.ar
** ARICANA
   Buenos Aires 934, 2000 Rosario, Argentina
   Tel: (41) 21-7664   Fax: (41) 21-9179
   E-mail: aricana@interactive.com.ar
** ATICANA
   Salta 581, 4000 San Miguel de Tucuman, Argentina
   Tel: (81) 31-0616   Fax: (81) 30-3070
   E-mail: aticana@starnet.net.ar
* American Training Co.
   Viamonte 577, Piso 7, 1053 Buenos Aires, Argentina
   Tel: (1) 311-3699   Fax: (1) 315-3573
Berlitz
   Av. de Mayo 847 1er Piso, 1084 Buenos Aires, Argentina
   Tel: (11) 4342-0202
   E-mail: info@berlitz.com.ar
Berlitz
   Av. del Libertador 15231, 1640 Acassuso, Argentina
   Tel: (11) 4747-1871   Fax: (11) 4732-3096
   E-mail: info@berlitz.com.ar
* Brooklyn Bridge
   Reconquista 715, 6 C y D, 1003 CF, Buenos Aires,
   Argentina

Tel: (1) 313-1652

* CAIT
  Av. Pte. Roque Saenz Pena 615, Piso 6, Of. 631, 1393
  Buenos Aires, Argentina
  Tel: (1) 326-3230   Fax: (1) 326-2926
  E-mail: cait@ciudad.com.ar
  Centum Servicios de Idiomas
  Bartolome Mitre, Piso 4, 1036 Buenos, Aires,
  Argentina
  Fax: (1) 328-5150
** ICANA
  Maipu 672, 1006 Buenos Aires, Argentina
  Tel: (1) 322-3855   Fax: (1) 322-2106
  E-mail: icana@bcl.edu.ar
** IDFICAA
  9 de Julio 177, 5200 Dean Funes, Cordoba, Argentina
  Tel: (51) 20-738   Fax: (51) 21-001
** IICANA
  Dean Funes 726, 5000 Cordoba, Argentina
  Tel: (51) 23-7858   Fax: (51) 23-7858
  E-mail: tarcher@satlink.com
* International House
  J. A. Pacheco de Melo 2555, 1425 CF, Buenos Aires,
  Argentina
  Tel: (114) 805-6393   Fax: (114) 801-5954
  E-mail: melo@internet.siscotel.com
  Website: www.ba.net/ihba/
* International House
  Cosme Beccar 225, 1642 San Isidro, Argentina
  Tel: (114) 743-2518
  E-mail: ihsanisi@sminter.com.ar
** IPICANA
  Lisandro de La Torre 674, 6300 Santa Rosa, La Pampa,
  Argentina
  Tel: (954) 53-356   Fax: (954) 32-606

Bolivia   591

** Centro Boliviano Americano
Calle 25 de Mayo N-0365, Casilla 1399, Cochabamba,
Bolivia
Tel: (42) 21-288   Fax: (42) 51-225
E-mail: suarezmj@llajta.nrc.bolnet.bo
** Centro Boliviano Americano
Parque Zenon Iturralde No. 121, Casilla 12024, La Paz,
Bolivia
Tel: (2) 43-0107   Fax: (2) 43-1342
E-mail: cbalp@datacom-bo.net
** Centro Boliviano Americano
C/. Cochabamba No. 66, Casilla 510, Santa Cruz de la
Sierra, Bolivia
Tel: (3) 34-2299   Fax: (3) 35-0188
E-mail: cbascz@datacom-bo.net
** Centro Boliviano Americano
C/. Calvo No. 331, Casilla No. 380, Sucre, Chuquisaca,
Bolivia
Tel: (64) 41-608   Fax: (64) 41-608
E-mail: cba@nch.bolnet.bo
Colegio San Calixto
C/. Jenaro Sanjines 701, La Paz, Bolivia
Tel: (2) 35-5278
Pan American English Center
Edificio Avenida, Av. 16 de Julio 1490, Piso 7, Casilla
5244, La Paz, Bolivia
Tel/Fax: (2) 34-0796

Brazil   55

** ACBEU
Avenida Sete de Setembro 1883, 40080-002 Salvador - BA,
Brazil
Tel: (71) 336-4411   Fax: (71) 245-9233
E-mail: acbeu@ufba.br

** Associacao Brasil-America
Avenida Malaquias 171, Aflitos, 52050-060 Recife - PE,
Brazil
Tel: (81) 241-7213   Fax: (81) 427-1881
E-mail: teresa@ababib.anpe.br

Berlitz
Av. Erico Verissimo 299, 22621-180 Rio de Janeiro, RJ,
Brazil
Tel: (21) 491-3748

Berlitz
R. Barao da Torre 559, 22411-000 Rio de Janeiro, RJ,
Brazil
Tel: (21) 512-3394   Fax: (21) 512-3448

Berlitz
R Haddock Lobo 1152, 01414-002 Sao Paulo, SP, Brazil
Tel: (11) 881-3877   Fax: (11) 881-3847

Berlitz
R. das Figueiras 1149, 09080-370 Sao Paulo, SP, Brazil
Tel: (11) 4979-4660

Brasas English Courses
Rua Voluntarios de Patria 190/315, Botafogo, 22270-010
Rio de Janeiro - RJ, Brazil
Tel: (21) 527-1838   Fax: (21) 286-8996
Website: www.brasas.com

* Britannia Schools   (Rio, Sao Paulo, Porto Alegre)
Av. Borges de Medeiros 67, Leblon, Rio de Janeiro, RJ,
Brazil
Tel: (21) 511-0143   Fax: (21) 511-0893
E-mail: sdmale@britannia.com.br
Website: www.britannia.com.br

* Britanic International House
Rua Hermogenes de Morais 163, Madalena 50 610-160,
Recife - PE, Brazil
Tel: (81) 445-5564   Fax: (81) 445-5481
E-mail: office@britanic-ih.com.br
Website: www.internationalhouse.com.br

Casa Branca

> Rua Machado de Assis 37, Boqueirao, Santos SP, 11050-060, Brazil
> Tel: (13) 233-5258
> E-mail: casabranca@atribuna.com.br

** Casa Thomas Jefferson

> SEP/Sul 706/906 Conjunto B, Caixa Postal 07-1201, 70390-065 Brasilia - DF, Brazil
> Tel: (61) 243-6588   Fax: (61) 243-8857
> E-mail: casatj@nutecnet.com.br

** CCBEU

> Trav. Padre Eutiquio 1309, Batista Campos, 66020-710 Belem - PA, Brazil
> Tel: (91) 242-4778   Fax: (91) 223-9455

** CCBEU

> Rua Amintas de Barros, 99, Edifico Itatiaia Centro, Caixa Postal 3328, 80060-200 Curitiba - PR, Brazil
> Tel: (41) 233-3422   Fax: (41) 232-2822

* ELC

> Rua Sae Souza 655, Boa Viagem, Recife PE, 51030-350, Brazil
> Fax: (81) 462-3244   E-mail: elc@elogica.com.br

ELS International

> Rua S. Peixoto 1255, 80240-120 Curitiba – PR, Brazil
> Tel: (41) 244-2605   Fax: (41) 243-8666
> E-mail: elscur@sul.com.br
> Website: elscuritiba.com

* English Forever

> Rua Rio Grande do Sol 356, Pituba, Salvador BA 41830-140, Brazil
> Fax: (71) 248-8706
> E-mail: forever@svn.com.br

* Evoluta

> Alameda Araguaia, 100 Centro Empresarial Alphaville, Barueri SP 06455-000, Brazil
> Tel: (011) 421-2766   E-mail: idiomas@evoluta.com.br

** IBEU
    Av. N. Sra. de Copacabana 690/6 11 andar, Copacabana,
    Caixa Postal 12.154, 22050-000 Rio de Janeiro - RJ, Brazil
    Tel: (21) 255-8332   Fax: (21) 255-9355
** IBEU-CE
    Rua Noguera Acioly 891, Aldeota, 60100-140 Fortaleza -
    CE, Brazil
    Tel: (85) 252-3633   Fax: (85) 252-1567
    E-mail: marco@ibeuce.com.br
** ICBEU
    Rua da Bahia 1723, Lourdes, 30160-011 Belo Horizonte -
    MG, Brazil
    Tel: (31) 271-7255   Fax: (31) 222-4282
    E-mail: icbgeral@icbeu.com.br
** ICBEU
    1114 Prof. Joao Candido, CEP 86 010 001 Londrina - PR,
    Brazil
    Tel: (43) 324-5372   Fax: (43) 324-7441
    E-mail: info@cultural-lda.org.br
** Instituto Cultural Brasil-Norteamericano
    Rua Riachuelo 1257, Centro, 90010-271 Porto Alegre - RS,
    Brazil
    Tel: (51) 225-2651   Fax: (51) 225-2255
* Instituto da Lingua Inglesa
    Av. Do CPA 157, Cuiaba MT, 78008-000, Brazil
    Tel: (65) 624-1197
    E-mail: insling@zaz.com.br
* International House Goiania
    Rua 4 n.80, Setor Oeste, Goiania - GO, 74110-170, Brazil
    Tel: (62) 224-0478   Fax: (62) 223-1846
    E-mail: inthouse@zaz.com.br
Liberty English Centre
    Rua Amintas de Barros 1059, Curitiba PR, 80060-200,
    Brazil
    Tel: (41) 263-3586   Fax: (41) 263-1738
    E-mail: liberty@cwbone.bsi.com.br

* M School
   Av. Marechal Rondon 745 C, Ji-Parana – Ro CEP, 78960-000, Brazil,
   Tel: (69) 422-3100   E-mail: mschool@pcnet.com.br
* RLC Schools
   SHIS Q1 05 Area Especial 01 Bloco "d" Centro Hangar 5, Lago Sul, Brasilia – DF CEP, 71615-530, Brazil
   Tel: (61) 364-1884
   E-mail: rlc.idiomas@zaz.com.br
* Seven English - Espanol
   Rua Antonio Carlos 319, Sao Paulo – SP CEP, 01309-011, Brazil
   Tel: (11) 285-4300
   E-mail: seven@sevenidiomas.com.br
Sharing English
   Rua Souza de Andrade56, 52050-300 Recife – PE, Brazil
   Tel: (81) 421-2286
* System 2000
   Rua Deputado Jose Lajes 491, Ponta Verde, Maceio AL, 57035-330, Brazil
   Tel: (82) 327-9911   Fax: (82) 327-3958
   E-mail: system@dialnet.com.br
* The Interstation
   Rua Goias 1507, Centro, Londrinas PR, 86020-340, Brazil
   Tel: (43) 323-7700
   E-mail: estation@sercomtel.com.br
** UNIAO
   Rua Colonel Oscar Porto 208, Paraiso, Caixa Postal 7197, 04003-000 Sao Paulo - SP, Brazil
   Tel: (11) 885-1022   Fax: (11) 885-0376
   E-mail: postmaster@uniao.com.br
* Upper English (San Carlos)
   Rua 09 de Julho 2143, Sao Carlos SP, 13560-590, Brazil
   Tel: (16) 271-8146
   E-mail: upperenglish@linkway.com.br

Chile   56

Berlitz
>   Cruz del Sur 88, Santiago, Chile
>   Tel: (2) 228-8679   Fax: (2) 206-1667
>   E-mail: paulina.soler@berlitz.cl

Berlitz
>   San Martin 516, Concepcion, Chile
>   Tel: (41) 23-9936   Fax: (41) 23-5007
>   E-mail: berlitz-biobio@entelchile.net

Berlitz
>   2 Norte 610, Vina del Mar, Chile
>   Tel: (32) 69-5660   Fax: (32) 69-5881
>   E-mail: cristian.reid@berlitz.cl

ELADI Instituto Profesional
>   Jose M. Infante 927, Providencia, Santiago, Chile
>   Fax: (2) 225-0958

ELS International
>   Fidel Oteiza 1956, Piso 16, Providencia, Santiago, Chile
>   Tel/Fax: (2) 343-9942   E-mail: elschile@ctcinternet.cl

Fischer English Institute
>   Cirujano Guzman 49, Providencia, Santiago, Chile
>   Fax: (2) 235-9810

IBC
>   Presidente Errazuriz 3328, Las Condes, Santiago,Chile
>   Fax: (2) 233-8143   E-mail: ibc@reuna.cl

Impact English
>   Rosa O'Higgins 259, Las Condes, Santiago, Chile
>   Tel: (2) 211-1925   Fax: (2) 211-6165

Instituto Chileno Britanico de Cultura
>   San Martin 531, Concepcion, Chile
>   Fax: (41) 234-044

** Instituto Chileno Norteamericano
>   Carrera 1445, Casilla P, Antofagasta, Chile
>   Tel: (55) 262-731   Fax: (55) 262-731
>   E-mail: chilnor@cobre.reuna.cl

** Instituto Chileno Norteamericano
Caupolican 315, Casilla 612, Concepcion, Chile
Tel: (41) 248-589   Fax: (41) 233-851
** Instituto Chileno Norteamericano
Moneda 1467, Casilla 9286, Santiago, Chile
Tel: (2) 232-6107   Fax: (2) 698-1175
E-mail: infocent@hood.ichn.cl
** Instituto Chileno Norteamericano
Esmeralda 1069, Casilla 1297, Valparaiso, Chile
Tel: (32) 255-725   Fax: (32) 255-725
E-mail: infocenv@hood.ichn.cl
* International House Santiago
Roman Diaz 292, Providencia, Santiago, Chile
E-mail: internationalhouse@ihsantiago.com
Website: ihsantiago.com
Let's Do English
Villa Vicencio 361, Of. 109, Santiago, Chile
Fax: (2) 633-8535
Polyglot
Villa Vicencio 361, Of. 102, Santiago, Chile
Fax: (2) 632-2485
E-mail: polyglot@santiago.cl
Web site: www.santiago.cl/polyglot
Tromwell
Apoquindo 4499, Piso 3, Las Condes, Santiago, Chile
Tel: (2) 246-1040   Fax: (2) 228-9739
Wall Street Institute
San Sebastian 2878, Comuna Condes, Santiago, Chile
Fax: (2) 332-0326

Colombia   57

** Centro Cultural Colombo Americano
Carrera 43, No. 51-95, Apt Aereo 2097, Barranquilla,
Colombia
Tel: (5) 340-8084   Fax: (5) 340-8549

E-mail: colombo@b-quilla.cetcol.net.co
** Centro Colombo Americano
   C/. 13 Norte # 8-45, Apartado Aereo 4525, Cali, Colombia
   Tel: (2) 668-1922   Fax: (2) 668-4695
   E-mail: cencolam@cali.cetcol.net.co
** Centro Colombo Americano
   C/. de la Factoria 36-27, Apt. Aereo 2831, Cartagena,
   Colombia
   Tel: (5) 664-0395   Fax: (5) 660-0415
** Centro Colombo Americano
   Carrera 45, # 53-24, Apt. Aereo 8734, Medellin, Colombia
   Tel: (4) 513-4444   Fax: (4) 513-2666
   E-mail: bncmde@medellin.cetcol.net.co
** Centro Colombo Americano
   Carrera 6, No. 22-26, Apt. Aereo 735, Pereira, Colombia
   Tel: (63) 336-465   Fax: (63) 354-291
   E-mail: colompei@eccel.com
Centro de Ingles Lincoln
   C/. 49, No. 9-37, Bogota, Colombia
   Tel: (1) 288-0360   Fax: (1) 287-3806
ELS International
   C/. 85 #11-78, Bogota, Colombia
   Tel: (1) 257=4602   Fax: (1) 257-4660
   E-mail: kjamboosels1@hotmail.com
ELS International
   Av. Roosevelt Transversal 5a, 5 E-80, Cali, Valle,
   Colombia
   Tel: (2) 553-6397   Fax: (2) 332-8426
   E-mail: lacenter@hotmail.com
First Class English
   Carrera 12, No. 93-78, Piso 4 M, Santa Fe de Bogota,
   Colombia
   Tel: (1) 623-2375   Fax: (1) 623-2379
International Language Institute,
   Cra. 13, No. 5-79, Castillo Grande, Cartagena, Colombia
   Tel: (5) 665-1672

Costa Rica 506

Berlitz - Centro Forum
> Frente a Santa Ana 2000, Edificio A, Planta Baja, Santa
> Ana, San Jose, Costa Rica
> Tel: 204-7555   Fax: 204-7444

** Centro Cultural Costarricense Norteamericano
> Apt. 1489-1000, San Jose, Calle Los Negritos, Barrio Dent,
> Costa Rica
> Tel: 225-6433   Fax: 224-1480
> E-mail: centrcr@sol.racsa.co.cr

Centro Linguistico
> Sra. Rita Salas, Apartado 151, Alajula, Costa Rica

EI S International
> Apartado 6495-1000, San Jose, Costa Rica
> Tel: 261-4242   Fax: 261-3212
> E-mail: acallen@uicr.ac.cr

Instituto Britanico
> P O Box 8184, San Jose 1000, Costa Rica
> Tel: 225-0256   Fax: 253-1894
> E-mail: instbrit@sol.racsa.co.cr

Instituto de Ingles USA
> Apartado 418-1002 C1 A6, San Jose, Costa Rica

* International Christian School
> Apartado 3512, San Jose, Costa Rica
> Tel: 236-7879   Fax: 235-1518
> E-mail: intchris@sol.racsa.co.cr

Lincoln School
> P O Box 1919, San Jose, Costa Rica
> Tel: 235-7733   Fax: 236-1706

Dominican Republic 809

Berlitz
> Av. 27 de Febrero #589, Santo Domingo, Dominican
> Republic
> Tel: 412-8770   Fax: 412-8785

E-mail: berlitz@tricom.net
** Instituto Cultural Dominico-Americano
　　Avenida Estrella Sadala, La Rinconada, Apartado 767,
　　Santiago de los Caballeros, Dominican Republic
　　Tel: 582-6627　　　　Fax: 587-3858
　　E-mail: d.mclean@codetel.net.do
** Instituto Cultural Dominico-Americano
　　Av. Abraham Lincoln No. 21, Santo Domingo, Dominican
　　Republic
　　Tel: 533-4191　　　　Fax: 533-8809

Ecuador　　　593

* Alpha English Programs
　　Salazar 427 y Coruna, Casilla 17-16-18, Quito, Ecuador
　　Tel: (2) 235-068　　　　E-mail: alpha@hoy.net
Benedict School of Languages
　　P O Box 09-01-8916, Guayaquil, Ecuador
　　Tel: (4) 444-418　　　　Fax: (4) 441-642
　　E-mail: benecent@telconet.net
Benedict School of Languages
　　Edmundo Chiriboga N47-133 y Jorge Paez, Quito, Ecuador
　　Tel: (2) 462-972　　　　Fax: (2) 432-729
　　E-mail: benedict@accessinter.net
CEDEI
　　Casilla 597, Cuenca, Ecuador
　　Tel: (7) 839-003　　　　Fax: (7) 833-593
　　E-mail: English@c.ecua.net.ec
** Centro Ecuatoriano Norteamericano Abraham Lincoln
　　Borrero 5-18, P.O. Box 01.01.1939, Cuenca, Ecuador
　　Tel: (7) 823-898　　　　Fax: (7) 841-737
　　E-mail: rboroto@cena.org.ec
** Centro Ecuatoriano Norteamericano Urdaneta y Codova
　　P.O. Box 09-01-5717, Guayaquil, Ecuador
　　Tel: (4) 326-505　　　　Fax: (4) 564-514
　　E-mail: susana@cen.org.ec

Experimento de Convivencia Internacional
> Hernando de la Cruz 218 y Mariana de Jesus, Quito,
> Ecuador
> Tel: (2) 551 937   Fax: (2) 550 228

* Key Language Services
> Foch 635 y Reina Victoria, Casilla 17-079770, Quito,
> Ecuador
> Tel/Fax: (2) 557 851
> E-mail: kls@hoy.net

* Lingua Franca
> Casilla 17-12-68, Edificio Jerico, 12 de Octobre 2449 y
> Orellana, Quito, Ecuador
> Tel: (2) 546 075   Fax: (2) 500 734

Nexus Lenguas y Culturas
> Jose Peralta 1-19 y 12 de Abril, Cuenca, Ecuador
> Tel: (7) 888 220   Fax: (7) 888 221
> E-mail: nexus@cue.satnet.net

South American Spanish Institute
> Amazonas 1549 y Santa Maria, Quito, Ecuador
> Fax: (2) 226 438
> E-mail: sudameri@impsat.net.ec

El Salvador   503

CIS MAM Language School
> Boulevard Universitario, Casa No. 4, San Salvador, El
> Salvador
> Tel/Fax: 226-2623

Guatemala   502

** Instituto Guatemalteco-Americano
> Ruta 1, 4-05, Zona 4, Apto.691, Guatemala City, Guate
> mala
> Tel: 331-0022   Fax: 332-3135
> E-mail: bibiga@infovia.com.gt

Modern American English
>> C/. de los Nazarenos 16, Antigua, Guatemala
>> Tel: 932-3306   Fax: 932-0217

** Institut Haitiano-Americain
>> Angle rue Capois et rue St. Cyr, Port-au-Prince, Haiti
>> Tel: 22-3715   Fax: 23-8324

Honduras   504

** Centro Cultural Sampedrano
>> 3 Calle, entre 3A y 4A Avenida #20, Apartado Postal 511,
>> San Pedro Sula, Cortes, Honduras
>> Tel: 57-2084   Fax: 57-8804

** Instituto Hondureno de Cultura Interamericana
>> 2 Avenida entre 5 y 6 Calles No. 520, Apartado 201,
>> Tegucigalpa, M.D.C. Comayaguela, Tegucigalpa,
>> Honduras
>> Tel: 37-7539   Fax: 38-0064

Mexico   52

Mexico is one of the biggest and most accessible TEFL markets for both trained and untrained Canadian and American teachers. Some jobs with language schools can be pre-arranged but most are arranged on arrival in the country.

Mexican universities frequently employ US/Canadian teachers who have either a MA TESOL or a recognized TEFL certificate, such as the RSA/Cambridge CELTA. Some university addresses are given below, but a comprehensive list, with hyperlinks, can be found at the following website: www.mexonline.com/univrsty.htm

* ACE - International House
>> World Trade Centre, Avenue de las Naciones No. 1,
>> Despacho 20-04, Col. Napoles 03810, Mexico City, Mexico
>> Tel/Fax: (5) 488-0223
>> E-mail: inthouse@www.bsmx.com

Teaching English Overseas

* American School of Tampico Language Institute
    E. Azcarraga 208 Sur, Col. Campbell 89260, Tampico,
    Tamaulipas, Mexico
    E-mail: lporozco@tamnet.com.mx
Arizona School of English
    Deco Plaza Santa Maria, Blvd. Rosales S/N L-23 Altos,
    Col. Centro, Los Mochis Sinaloa, Mexico
    Tel: (68) 18 56 71
Berlitz
    Av. Montevideo 365, Esq. Payta, Col. Lindavista, 07300,
    Mexico D.F.
    Tel: (57) 52 12 10   Fax: (57) 54 40 25
    E-mail: centro.lindavista@berlitz.com.mx
Berlitz
    Plaza Las Flores, Loc. 4 y 5, Av. Uxmal #77 Sm Mz 16,
    Cancun, Quintana Roo, Mexico
    Tel: (98) 87 91 44
Berlitz
    Av. Domingo Diez #1460, Loc. 21, Col. San Cristobal,
    62630 Cuernavaca Morelos, Mexico
    Tel: (7) 317-6170
    E-mail: berlitzc@netcall.com.mx
Berlitz
    Pablo Neruda #2914, Col. Providencia, 44260 Guadalajara,
    Mexico
    Tel: (3) 641-4048   Fax: (3) 641-2768
Berlitz
    Blvd. Ruiz Cortones #1600, Fracc. Costa de Oro, Boca Del
    Rio, Veracruz, Mexico
    Tel: (29) 22 76 66   Fax: (29) 22 76 68
Culturlingua
    Plaza Las Palomas 30, C.P. 59680, Zamora, Michoacan,
    Mexico
    Tel/Fax: (351) 53 616
    E-mail: azschool@yahoo.com
    Website: http://members.tripod.com/~azschool/

Harmon Hall
  Huichapan esq. Tizayuca, Col. Rojo Gomez 43990 CD,
  Sahagun, HGO, Mexico
  Tel/Fax: (596) 33 818
** Centro Mexicano Americano de Relaciones Culturales
  Xola 416, Colonia del Valle, 03100 Mexico, D.F., Mexico
  Tel (5) 536-5520   Fax: (5) 536-1467
  E-mail: cemarc@sisisa.podernet.com.mx
  Web Site: http://www.ciudadempresarial.com.mx
** Instituto Cultural Mexicano-Norteamericano de Jalisco
  Av. Enrique Diaz de Leon Sur #300, 44100 Guadalajara,
  Jalisco, Mexico
  Tel: (3) 825-5838   Fax: (3) 825-1671
  E-mail: cultural@acnet.net
** Instituto Mexicano Americano de Relaciones Culturales
  Blvd. Navarrete y Monteverde, Hermosillo, Sonora,
  Mexico
  Tel: (621) 40 781
** Instituto Franklin de Yucatan
  Calle 57, No. 474-A, 97000 Merida, Yucatan, Mexico
  Tel: (99) 21 5996   Fax: (99) 27 2700
  E-mail: franklin@pibil.finred.com.mx
** Instituto Mexicano-NorteAmericano de Relaciones Culturales
  Hidalgo 768 Pte., 64000 Monterrey, Nuevo Leon, Mexico
  Tel: (8) 340-1583   Fax: (8) 345-1988
  E-mail: bibbfranc@intercable.net
** Instituto Mexicano-Norteamericano
  Guillermo Prieto 86, 58000 Morelia, Michoacan, Mexico
  Tel: (43) 12 4112   Fax: (43) 12 5153
** Instituto Mexicano Norteamericano de Relaciones Culturales
  Jose Santos Chocano #606, Col. Anahuac, 66450 San
  Nicolas de los Garza, Nuevo Leon, Mexico
  Tel: (8) 376-7692   Fax: (8) 376-5187
** Instituto Franklin de Veracruz
  Azueta 1229 & Diaz Miron, Veracruz, Veracruz, Mexico
  Tel: (29) 31 5736

MCCI (Schools in San Luis Potosi and Queretara)
Juan de Onate 660, San Luis Potosi, Mexico 78270
E-mail: mcci@slp.1.telmex.net.mx
* Universidad Autonoma de Baja California Sur
Carretera al Sur Km 5.5, 23080 La Paz, BCS, Mexico
Tel: (1) 128-0440
Website: www.uabcs.mx
* Universidad Autonoma de Campeche
Fac. de Humanidades, Av. Universidad X Agustin Melgar,
Col. Lindavista, Campeche, Com. CP 24030, Mexico
Tel: (981) 67-208
Website: www.uacam.mx

Nicaragua   505

** Centro Cultural Nicaraguense-NorteAmericano
Centro Comercial Nejapa, Managua, Nicaragua
Tel: (2) 653-038   Fax: (2) 652-727
E-mail: ccnn@uugate.uni.edu.ni

Panama   507

** Centro Pan-USA
Balboa, Roosevelt Ave. Bldg.635, Panama City, Panama
Tel: 232-6718   Fax: 232-7292
E-mail: panusa@sinfo.net
ELS Language Center
Urb. Obarrio, Calle 54 Este, #23, Panama City, Panama
Tel: 264-0924   Fax: 214-9137
E-mail: alberto@els.edu.pa

Paraguay   595

** Centro Cultural Paraguayo-Americano
Avenida Espana 352, Asuncion, Paraguay
Fax:(21) 226-133   E-mail: ccpa@sce.cnc.una.py

Peru   51

Berlitz
Av. Santa Cruz 236, San Isidro, Lima 27, Peru
Tel: (1) 440-8077   Fax: (1) 441-7225
Berlitz
Av. Javier Prado Este 5001, Camacho, La Molina, Peru
Tel: (1) 434-4851
Foster & Foster Private Institute
Miguel Dasso 139-301 San Isidro, Lima, Peru
Tel: (1) 949-1902   Fax: (1) 442-7520
** ICPNA
Melgar 109, Apartado 555, Arequipa, Peru
Tel: (54) 243-201   Fax: (54) 237-731
E-mail: jrivera@LaRed.net.pe
** ICPNA
Manuel M. Izaga 807, Apartado 34, Chiclayo, Peru
Tel: (74) 231-241   Fax: (74) 227-166
E-mail: icpnachi@mail.udep.edu.pe
** ICPNA
Av. Tullumayo 125, Apartado 287, Cusco, Peru
Tel: (84) 224-112   Fax: (84) 233-541
E-mail: oicpnacus+@qenqo.rcp.net.pe
** ICPNA
Jr. Guido 754, Apartado 624, Huancayo, Peru
Tel: (64) 224-152   Fax: (64) 232-141
E-mail: icpnahyo@correo.dnet.com.pe
** ICPNA
Jr. Cusco 446, Apartado 304, Lima, Peru
Tel: (1) 428-3530   Fax: (1) 427-0797
E-mail: pcanales@icpna.edu.pe
** ICPNA
Apurimac 447, Piura, Peru
Tel: (74) 331-360
E-mail: icpna-rg@lanet.com.pe

** ICPNA

Av. Venezuela 125 esq. Husares de Junin, Trujillo, Peru
Tel: (44) 232-512   Fax: (44) 261-922

Instituto de Idiomas
Camino Real 1037, San Isidro, Lima 27, Peru
Tel: (1) 441-5962

William Shakespeare Institute
Avenida Dos de Mayo 1105, San Isidro, Lima, Peru
Tel: (14) 440-1004   Fax: (14) 422-1313

Uruguay   598

** Alianza Cultural Uruguay-Estados Unidos de America
C/. Paraguay 1217, Canelones 1069, Montevideo, Uruguay
Tel: (2) 902-5160   Fax: (2) 920-5165

Berlitz
Bvar. Gral. Artigas 1253, Montevideo, Uruguay
Tel: (2) 403-0121   Fax: (2) 408-6729

CEDI   (5 schools)
Bvar. Artigas 2293, Montevideo, Uruguay
Tel: 230-257

* Dickens Institute   (3 schools)
21 de Setiembre 3090, Montevideo, Uruguay
Tel: 700-346

* English Studies Centre
Obligado 1221, Montevideo, Uruguay
Tel: 783-751

* International House / London Institute
Av. Brasil 2831, Montevideo, 11300 Uruguay
E-mail: araz@netgame.com.uy

Millington Drake Institute   (5 schools)
Michigan 1710B, Montevideo, Uruguay
Tel: 630-205

Queen Victoria Institute
Libertad 2791, Montevideo, Uruguay
Tel: 780-943

Venezuela 58

Berlitz
Centro Las Mercedes, C/. Madrid, Quinta Manuela, 1060 Caracas, Venezuela
Tel: (2) 993-5574   Fax: (2) 993-6851
** CVA
Casilla 61715 de Este, Caracas 1060A, Venezuela
Tel: (2) 993-7911   Fax: (2) 993-8422
** CEVAZ
C/. 63, 3E-60, Apt. 419, Maracaibo, Edo. Zulia, Venezuela
Tel: (61) 91-1880   Fax: (61) 92-1098
** CEVAM
Apt. Postal 27, La Parroquia, Merida 5115 A, Venezuela
Tel: (74) 63-1362   Fax: (74) 63-1490
E-mail: cevam@ing.ula.ve
English Lab
Apt. Postal 4004, Carmelitas, Caracas 1101, Venezuela
Tel: (2) 574-2511   Fax: (2) 573-2631
ESJ
Av. Libertador, Res. Florida, Apto. 5, La Florida, Venezuela
Tel: (2) 712-069
Iowa Institute
Ubicacion Av. Cuatro con C/. 18, Merida, Venezuela
Tel: (74) 526-404
Loscher Ebbinhaus
La Trinidad, C/. San Jose, Quinta Katerine, Sorocaima, Venezuela
Tel: (2) 932-459
Loscher Ebbinhaus
La Campina, Centro Comercial Av. Libertador, Crn. C/. Negrin (Piso 2), Caracas, Venezuela
Tel: (2) 762-5501   Fax: (2) 713-680
Wall Street Institute
Avenida Francisco de Miranda, Torre Lido piso 11, El Rosal, Caracas, Venezuela
Tel: (2) 953-7473

Wall Street Institute
>Centro Comercial Reda Building, Torre A, PB, Local #1,
>Las 4 Avenidas Del Parral Estado Carabobo, Valencia,
>Venezuela
>Tel: (41) 252-737   Fax: (41) 254-859

Wall Street Institute
>Av. Francisco de Miranda, Edif. Parque Cristal, Nivel
>Mezzanina Local LCC1-30, Caracas Los Palos Grandes,
>Venezuela
>Tel: (2) 285-0869   Fax: (2) 285-4250

MID EAST & TURKEY

THE MID EAST

Most of the TEFL jobs in the region are located in Arabian Gulf countries of Saudi Arabia, Kuwait and the United Arab Emirates.

In the case of Arabian Gulf countries, jobs have to be arranged in advance, with employers arranging and paying for visas, airfare and accommodations. Employers normally require teachers to have TEFL/ TESL training. Salaries are generally good and permit savings of $1000-$1500 a month. Teachers throughout the region live very comfortably in terms of amenities, utilities, etc. but entertainment opportunities are extremely limited. This is particularly true of Saudi Arabia, where many teachers live and work on military or company compounds.

There are good employment opportunities for both men and women in Kuwait and the UAE. Women can teach in Saudi Arabia but they are subject to a great many restrictions.

A few jobs are available with US-run organizations in Jordan and Syria. Some of these positions can be arranged from North America, but employers rarely pay airfare. Salaries allow a comfortable lifestyle but do not permit the kind of savings possible in the Gulf.

The following organizations frequently recruit EFL teachers for positions in various countries in the region:

AMIDEAST (Mid East)
      1730 M Street NW, Suite 1100, Washington, DC 20036-
      4505, USA
      Fax: (202) 766-7062
      E-mail: dduncan@amideast.org
Booz Allen Hamilton (Mid East)
      1725 Jefferson Davis Hwy., # 1100, Arlington, VA 22202,
      USA
      Tel: (703) 769-7700   Fax: (703) 892-4817
      E-mail: riveraalc@bah.com
      Website: www.bah.com

ELS Language Centers (Mid East)
    P O Box 3079, Abu Dhabi, UAE
    Tel: (971) (2) 651-516   Fax: (971) (2) 653-165
    E-mail: Elsme@emirates.net.ae
Robert Ventre Associates, Inc. (Mid East)
    22 Wharf Lane, Haverhill, MA 01830-1823, USA
    E-mail: Robert4559@aol.com

Bahrain   973

* The British Council
    Sheikh Salman Highway, P O Box 452, Manama, Bahrain
    Tel: 261-555   Fax: 258-689
Global Institute
    P O Box 11148, Manama, Bahrain
    Tel: 740-940   Fax: 720-030
Gulf School of Languages
    P O Box 20236, Manama, Bahrain
    Tel: 290-209   Fax: 290-069
Polyglot School
    P O Box 596, Manama, Bahrain
    Tel: 271-722   Fax: 273-050

Israel   972

Berlitz
    Hutzot Hamifratz, Vulcan Junction, Haifa Bay 26119,
    Israel
    Tel: (4) 872-7797   Fax: (4) 872-7799
Berlitz
    21 King George Street, Jerusalem 94261, Israel
    Tel: 223-6288   Fax: 223-6291
Berlitz
    Europe House, 37 Shaul Hamelech Ave., Tel Aviv 64298,
    Israel
    Tel: (3) 695-2131   Fax: (3) 695-2134

Jordan   **962**

American Language Center
P O Box 676, Abdoun 11118, Amman, Jordan
Tel: (6) 585-9102   Fax: (6) 585-9101
E-mail: JLuce@alc.edu.jo
Yarmouk Cultural Centre
P O Box 960312, Amman, Jordan
Tel: (6) 671-447

Kuwait   **965**

Berlitz
P O Box 29950, Safat, Kuwait 13160
Tel: 254-4443   Fax: 254-5495
E-mail: kuwaittseen@kuwait.chamber.com.kw
ELS International
Sulaiman Commercial Center, Hamad Al Mubarak Street,
P O Box 5104, Salmiya 22062, Kuwait
Tel: 572-2522   Fax: 573-3005

Oman   **968**

Al-Ghosnain Training Institute
P O Box 1016, Ruwi 114, Oman
Tel: 601-102   Fax: 605-521
Website: www.weboman.com/ghosnain
* Polyglot Institute
P O Box 221, Ruwi, Oman
Tel: 701-261   Fax: 794-602

Qatar   **974**

ELS Language Center
P O Box 22678, 56 Jaber bin Ghaith, Doha, Qatar
Tel: 699-223   Fax: 685-519
E-mail: elsdoha@qatar.net.qa

Saudi Arabia   966

ARAMCO
>   Foreign Service Employment, P O Box 4530, Houston, TX
>   77210, USA
>   Tel: (713) 432-4014

Hassan A. K. Algahtani Sons Co.
>   C/o Cheryl Ryan, 1187 Coast Village Rd., #1-164, Santa
>   Barbara, CA 93108, USA
>   Fax: (805) 966-3974
>   E-mail: cryan@saudijobs.com
>   Website: www.saudijobs.com

Elite Training Services
>   P O Box 11015, Jubail Industrial City 31961,
>   Saudi Arabia
>   Tel: (3) 341-5514   Fax: (3) 341-1336

ELS Language Center
>   P O Box 17746, Riyadh Plaza, Thalia Street, Jeddah
>   21494, Saudi Arabia
>   Tel: (2) 663-7536   Fax: (2) 663-6655
>   E-mail: elslc@naseej.com.sa

ELS Language Center
>   Al Orubah Plaza (4024), King Fahad Road, P O Box
>   57967, Riyadh 11584, Saudi Arabia
>   Tel: (1) 419-4114   Fax: (1) 419-2342
>   E-mail: fksaudia@khaleej.net.bh

* European Centre for Languages & Training
>   P O Box 60617, Riyadh 11555, Saudi Arabia
>   Tel: (1) 476-1218   Fax: (1) 479-3328
>   E-mail: anojaim@compuserve.com

* International House Dhahran
>   IIMIT, P.O. Box 38838, Doha Area 31942,
>   Dhahran, Saudi Arabia
>   E-mail: iimit@sahara.com.sa
>   Website: iimit.com

Syria   963

American Language Center
P O Box 29, Rawda Circle, Damascus, Syria
Tel: (11) 332-7236   Fax: (11) 331-9327

United Arab Emirates   971

Berlitz
P O Box 7993, Zayed the First Street, Bin Haiyai Building,
Abu Dhabi, UAE
Tel: (2) 672-287   Fax: (2) 672-289
E-mail: berlitz@emirates.net.ae
ELS International
P O Box 3079, Al Khaleej Al Arabi St., Abu Dhabi, UAE
Tel: (2) 669-225   Fax: (2) 653-165
E-mail: elsiauh@ns2.emirates.net.ae
ELS International
P O Box 2380, Al Garhoud Area, Villa #14, Street #20,
Dubai, UAE
Tel: (4) 827-616   Fax: (4) 827-861
E-mail: dbxels@emirates.net.ae
ELS International
P O Box 1496, Al Jimy Area, Al Ain, UAE
Tel: (3) 623-468   Fax: (3) 623-265
E-mail: elsaa@emirates.net.ae

Yemen   967

* Modern American Language Institute (MALI)
P O Box 11727, Sana`a, Republic of Yemen
Tel/Fax: (1) 241-561   E-mail: mali1@y.net.ye
Yemen-America Language Institute
P O Box 22347, Sana`a, Republic of Yemen
Tel: (1) 203-429   Fax: (1) 203-251
E-mail: info@yali.org.ye

TURKEY

Expatriate teachers of EFL have long been drawn to Turkey because of the country's rich diversity of culture, history and ecology, as well as its proximity to the Balkans, the Mid East and North Africa. Turkey offers a large number of job opportunities for both male and female teachers. Untrained teachers can usually find jobs from within Turkey, provided that they have a BA or BS degree. Trained teachers, preferably also with a degree, can arrange positions in advance or on the spot. Employers who recruit teachers from North America will sometimes pay all or part of the teachers' airfare. They will normally also arrange (but not pay for) accommodations.

Most jobs are in either Istanbul or Ankara, both of which are large, busy cities which offer foreigners plenty of excitement and entertainments. Some jobs are available in smaller cities (such as Izmir), which offer a quieter and more relaxed lifestyle.

It should be noted that although almost all Turks are Muslims, the state itself is nonsectarian and so foreigners are subject to many fewer restrictions than in the Mid East or North Africa.

Teachers normally work five days and 20-25 hours a week and often receive several weeks of paid vacation. Salaries permit a reasonably comfortable lifestyle but not significant savings. Turkey tends to suffer from periodic bouts of high inflation. During these periods, the standard of living of expatriate teachers can drop dramatically unless their contract provides for inflation-linked salary increases.

Turkey   90

Active English
        Ataturk Bulvari 127/701, Selcan Han. Bakanlikar, 06640
        Ankara, Turkey
        Tel: (312) 418-7973   Fax: (312) 425-8235
Antik English (3 schools in Istanbul)
        Kirmizi Sebboy Sok. No. 10, Istanbul Cad., Bakirkoy,
        Istanbul, Turkey
        Tel: (212) 570-4847   Fax: (212) 583-7934

E-mail: ANTIK@prizma.net
* Best English
Bayindir Sokak No. 53, Kizilay, Ankara, Turkey
Tel: (312) 417-1819   Fax: (312) 417-6808
E-mail: besteng@alnet.net
* British English (3 schools in Istanbul)
Cami Duragi Palazoglu Sok. No. 12/2-3-4-5-6, Sisli,
Istanbul, Turkey
Tel/Fax: (216) 418-8982
* Dilko English (4 schools in Istambul)
Hatboyu Caddesi No. 16, 34720 Bakirkoy, Istanbul,
Turkey
Tel: (212) 570-1270   Fax: (212) 543-6123
E-mail: dilko@superonline.com
* The English Centre
Selanik Caddesi No. 8, Kat. 5, Kizilay, Ankara, Turkey
Tel: (312) 435-3094   Fax: (312) 434-2738
* The English Centre
Rumeli Caddesi 92, Zeki Bey Apt. 4, Osmanbey, Istanbul,
Turkey
Tel: (212) 247-0983
E-mail: englishcentre@superonline.com
* The English Centre
Cum. Bulvari 125, Kat. 1/D/1, Alsancak, Izmir, Turkey
Tel: (232) 463-8487   Fax: (232) 464-3144
English Fast (5 schools in Ankara, Istanbul and Izmir)
Zuhuratbba Cad. 42, Bakirkoy, Istanbul, Turkey
Fax: (212) 561-3231
Evrim School of Languages
Cengiz Topel Caddesi 8, Camlibel, 33010 Mersin, Turkey
Tel: (324) 233-9541   Fax: (324) 237-0862
* Interlang (3 branches in Istanbul)
Istanbul Cad., Halkci Sok, Yalcinlar Han. No. 4, Bakirkoy,
Istanbul, Turkey
Tel: (212) 543-5795   Fax: (212) 542-7854

* Karizma / International House
  Nispetiye Cad Erdolen Ishani No. 38, Kat. 1, 1 Levent,
  80660 Istanbul, Turkey
  Tel: (212) 282-9064   Fax: (212) 282-3218
  E-mail: karizma_ltd@turk.net
  Website: www.ihistanbul.com
* Kent English (Branches in Ankara, Bolu and Istanbul)
  Mithatpasa Caddesi No. 46, Kat. 3-4-5, 06420 Kizilay,
  Ankara, Turkey
  Tel: (312) 434-3833   Fax: (312) 435-7334
  E-mail: kenteng@hitit.ato.org.tr
** Turkish-American Association
  Cennah Caddesi 20, 06690 Kavaklidere, Ankara, Turkey
  Tel: (312) 426-3727   Fax: (312) 468-2538
** Turkish-American Association
  Resat Bey Mahallesi 5, Yeni Yarbasi Karakolu Sokagi No.
  27, Adana, Turkey
  Tel: (322) 454-4345   Fax: (322) 457-6591
** Turkish-American Association
  1379 Sok. No. 39, Alsancak, Izmir, Turkey
  Tel: (232) 215-206   Fax: (232) 463-6411

Postscript

I hope that this book has helped you see how to take advantage of the many TEFL job opportunities which exist around the world. I hope too that the information and advice contained in it will help you to avoid the problems which befall many people who enter the field of teaching English overseas without doing sufficient research.

I myself have been working in TEFL for over 30 years, sometimes in quite difficult contexts and countries. I cannot truthfully say that I have enjoyed every single minute in every job or every country! However, I can say that I have never regretted my career choice, and that for me the many rewards of TEFL have definitely outweighed the problems. I sincerely hope that however much time you choose to spend in TEFL is equally rewarding.

If you have any comments on this book or any questions which I may be able to answer, please feel free to e-mail me (EngIntSF@aol.com).

Good luck!

Jeff Mohamed

English International
Distance Courses

Introductory Certificate in TEFL

This 50-hour distance course provides an excellent introduction to TEFL classroom management and teaching techniques. The techniques are clearly demonstrated in video-recorded excerpts of actual lessons. The course will also help you to improve your knowledge of American English grammar and to carry out a successful job search.

All participants who successfully complete a series of written assignments are awarded our "Introductory Certificate in TEFL."

Certificate in TEFL

People who have completed our Introductory Certificate course may take a special 50-hour extension course to obtain our "Certificate in TEFL." When combined, these two courses provide detailed training in all of the major aspects of TEFL: classroom management, TEFL techniques and materials, language development and job searching.

All participants who successfully complete a series of written assignments receive our "Certificate in TEFL."

Certificate in TEFL (with Practice Teaching)

This distance course is based on our "Certificate in TEFL" course but it also includes evaluated practice teaching. Course participants arrange to teach and video-record six hours of EFL classes. The recordings are then mailed to English International, where each lesson is personally critiqued and evaluated by Jeff Mohamed.

Every participant who attains the required standard in written assignments and practice teaching is awarded a full "Certificate in TEFL (with Practice Teaching)." This certificate is equivalent to a TEFL certificate gained by completing a 4-week intensive on-site training course.

English International Publications

"Teaching English Overseas" by Jeff Mohamed

This is the most comprehensive, up-to-date and informative TEFL job guide for Canadians and Americans.

"A Grammar Development Course For American Teachers of EFL/ ESL" by Jeff Mohamed

Based on a series of practical tasks, this self-study book will help you to improve your knowledge and awareness of American English grammar.

For more details of our TEFL publications and distance courses, please visit our website or contact us by e-mail:

Website: www.english-international.com

E-mail: EngIntSF@aol.com

AGMV Marquis

MEMBER OF SCABRINI MEDIA

Quebec, Canada
2005

Printed in Canada